NEW MEXICO'S
LIVING LANDSCAPES

A ROADSIDE VIEW

William W. Dunmire

Photography by
Christine Bauman and William W. Dunmire

Museum of New Mexico Press   Santa Fe

CONTENTS

INTRODUCTION

Snow in the high country east of Farmington. CCB

W HEN NEW MEXICANS SPEAK of our state's diversity, we typically talk about its people, for New Mexico can legitimately claim to be the most culturally diverse state in the nation. After all, nearly half our residents are of Hispanic heritage, many of them descendants from the original Spanish colonists. Roughly forty percent are Anglos, nearly one out of ten is American Indian, and the rest are a mixture of the world's ethnic groups and racial mixes. Indeed, twenty-two different Indian tribes still reside on the land of their ancestors; they include nineteen Pueblo cultures, two Apache tribes, and the Navajo Nation. New Mexicans are rightfully proud of their cultural diversity.

However, this book speaks to another kind of diversity—that of the natural world. For starters, New Mexico is geographically connected to five different ecological communities in North America. Elevations in our state, the fifth largest in the nation, range from 2,841 feet where the Pecos River flows out of New Mexico to 13,161 feet at the snowy summit of Wheeler Peak far to the north. Such a spread results in large climate variation—in both temperature and precipitation. A gamut of geological substrates and soil types provide a wide range of growing conditions for plants. The combination of these attributes results in our state being ranked close to the top in degree of natural diversity among the fifty states. Only California and Texas significantly exceed us in this category.

(previous)
The Organ Mountains. CCB

So it comes as no surprise to learn that our landscapes are wonderfully varied—ranging from vast rose-colored deserts that contrast with expanses of native grasslands, to endless mesas and escarpments, fresh black lava flows, and rugged, sometimes snowcapped mountains. It's a fact that more than nine-tenths of the state's land base remains in native or near native condition, providing landscapes that pulse from the effects of unpredictable weather and other natural cycles rather than from human manipulation. Ours truly are living landscapes.

The purpose of this book is to give readers an understanding of the natural elements that define the outdoor environment in each of the different regions of New Mexico and to focus on some of our most interesting landscape features. We often hear questions like "Why does the countryside around Las Cruces appear to be so different from that surrounding Albuquerque, Taos, or Farmington?" The answers to such questions will be found here.

Though many of my own fondest outdoor experiences have involved hiking into the backcountry and exploring our most remote wilderness settings, New Mexico's Living Landscapes will not take you along trails to those places. Instead, we will follow the paved highways that travel through some of the most captivating scenery in the Southwest.

But this is not meant to be a guidebook, and it isn't organized by driving routes. Nor will it give directions to particular landscape features, although the maps will help you locate many of the special places described in the text or portrayed in the photographs. Throughout the book the focus will be on the major ecoregions of the state.

By the term "ecoregion," I mean a large expanse of land containing distinctive natural communities of vegetation and animal life that have resulted from environmental conditions prevailing there over a long period of time. Ecoregions ignore state or other political borders and don't have sharp boundaries. In fact, all of New Mexico's major ecoregions are extensions of ecoregions that encompass far more land in other states and in Mexico than they do here.

New Mexico embraces two very different desert ecoregions—the Chihuahuan Desert, which projects up from northern Mexico; and the Great Basin Desert, whose boundaries spill over from Nevada, Utah, and Arizona into the northwest corner of the state. The Great Plains Grassland covering the eastern prairies and the Great Basin Grassland occupying the middle Rio Grande Valley and points west comprise our two grassland ecoregions. The Southern Rockies ecoregion that occupies much of Colorado extends south into New Mexico on the east side of the Rio Grande almost to the Sandia Mountains that tower over Albuquerque. However, since nearly all mountain ranges in New Mexico display similar plant and animal communities, in this book I use the term "Montane Forests" in describing our high-mountain forests and alpine

*Wildflowers and Mesquite in
the Chihuahuan Desert. CCB*

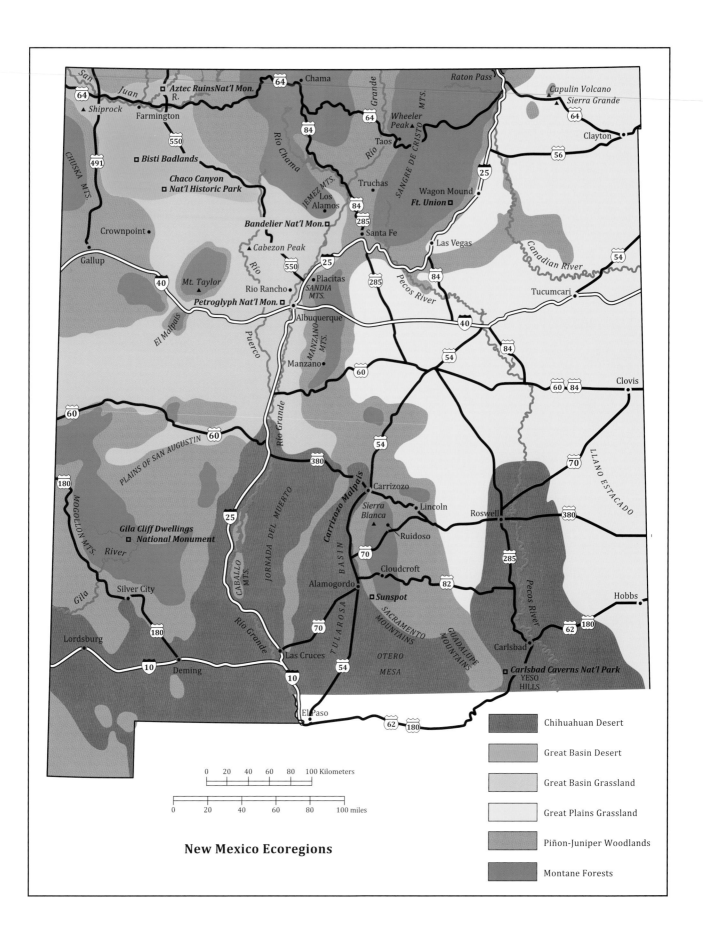

New Mexico Ecoregions

0   20   40   60   80   100 Kilometers

0   20   40   60   80   100 miles

Chihuahuan Desert

Great Basin Desert

Great Basin Grassland

Great Plains Grassland

Piñon-Juniper Woodlands

Montane Forests

zones and the term "Piñon-Juniper Woodlands" for land at the base of the mountains and on the plains where those two somewhat scruffy-looking trees dominate the scene. Threading through the several ecoregions are riparian corridors—rivers and streams—along with a number of lakes, all of which support distinctive wetland vegetation and animal life.

We will cover these ecoregions one by one in separate chapters, starting with our two deserts, followed by the two major grasslands, and, finally, the woodlands and forests above them. Riparian corridors contained within each region will be included in those chapters.

A number of the state's designated National and State Scenic Byways that course through individual ecoregions and provide good examples of them are described at the end of each chapter. Two scenic byways that cross ecoregion boundaries are portrayed in a separate chapter at the end of the book.

1 CHIHUAHUAN DESERT

FIRST
IMPRESSIONS

The Organ Mountains tower over Las Cruces; Claret-cup Cactus brightens the desert. CCB

TRAVELERS DRIVING into the Chihuahuan Desert for the first time can't help noticing how dry everything looks and how scarce trees seem to be, for this desert is mainly vegetated by shrubs and grasses. If your visit follows a rainy period in late spring or early summer, you may be treated to a marvelous display of wildflowers and blooming cacti. But even when few shrubs or wild-flowers are blossoming, you'll gradually discover that this is a land of highly varied but muted colors. That's due to the many shades of orange, pink, tan, and darker hues of the rocky slopes and soil wherever raw earth is exposed.

Although most of the terrain is flat or gently sloping, arid mountain ranges are almost always within distant view, and dry arroyos or washes regularly break up the flat expanses. In fact, you probably will be struck by how the Chihuahuan Desert tends to be rocky and somewhat barren.

Among the many varieties of large and small cacti and a number of the shrubby plants, spines are ever ready to prick the unwary. Most of the shrubs here are evergreen, so this desert has a somewhat similar appearance during every season of the year.

Be prepared for intense heat in summer and freezing temperatures in winter whenever a cold front passes through. Most days are cloudless or nearly so. In sum, you'll find the Chihuahuan Desert to be richly varied, dry, hot, and colorful—and full of delightful surprises.

Las Cruces, Carlsbad, and Alamogordo are the major cities that have been settled in the Chihuahuan Desert north of the border.

(previous)
White Sands. CCB

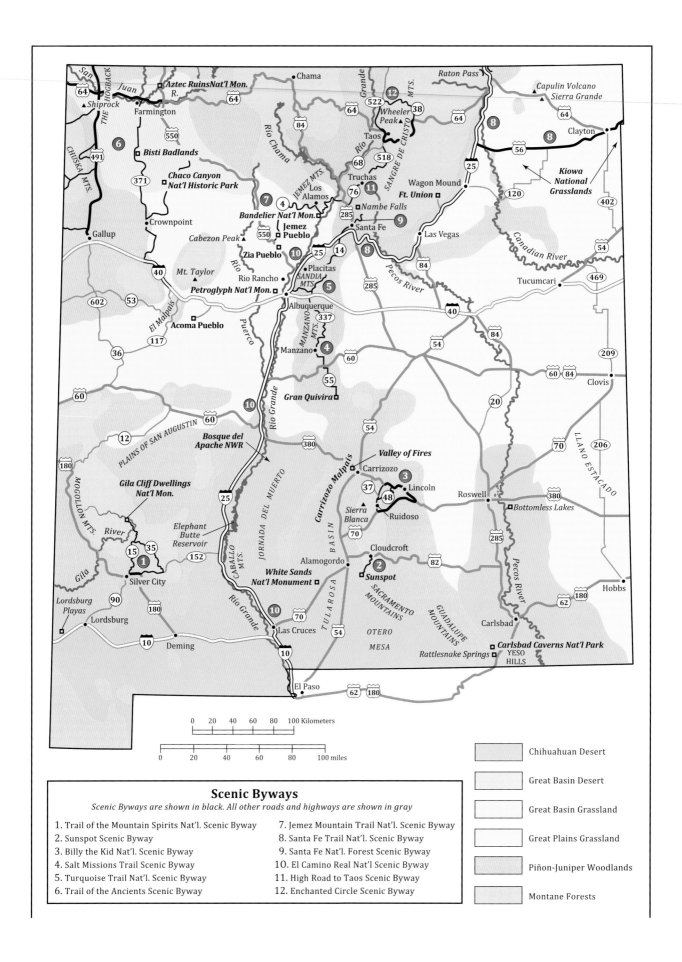

Scenic Byways

Scenic Byways are shown in black. All other roads and highways are shown in gray

1. Trail of the Mountain Spirits Nat'l. Scenic Byway
2. Sunspot Scenic Byway
3. Billy the Kid Nat'l. Scenic Byway
4. Salt Missions Trail Scenic Byway
5. Turquoise Trail Nat'l. Scenic Byway
6. Trail of the Ancients Scenic Byway
7. Jemez Mountain Trail Nat'l. Scenic Byway
8. Santa Fe Trail Nat'l. Scenic Byway
9. Santa Fe Nat'l. Forest Scenic Byway
10. El Camino Real Nat'l Scenic Byway
11. High Road to Taos Scenic Byway
12. Enchanted Circle Scenic Byway

Chihuahuan Desert

Great Basin Desert

Great Basin Grassland

Great Plains Grassland

Piñon-Juniper Woodlands

Montane Forests

OCCUPYING MORE LAND than the entire state of California, the Chihuahuan Desert is North America's largest arid landscape. Most of the roughly two hundred thousand square miles of this desert lies south of our border, but it extends northward into southwest Texas and southern New Mexico and barely sneaks across our southwestern border into eastern Arizona. Most of the southern third of New Mexico is classed as Chihuahuan Desert, and a finger of the desert extends north on either side of the Rio Grande beyond Socorro, nearly to Albuquerque.

Like almost all deserts, the Chihuahuan is hot throughout the summer, with temperatures reaching well above one hundred degrees Fahrenheit on many or most days, but winter weather tends to be cooler than in many of the other major deserts in the world. For example, in Las Cruces during a typical year temperatures plunge below freezing on many nights, and at least one snowstorm will occur. Although annual rainfall averages only ten inches, that's a good deal wetter than is typical of the other three deserts in the western United States.

According to the World Wide Fund for Nature, the Chihuahuan may be the most biologically diverse desert in the world when it comes to the variety of plant and animal life. Part of the reason is that so many different habitats have developed here under the influence of large variations in elevation, an ample assortment of soil types, and the fact that, though not always apparent to the traveler, springs and seeps are relatively plentiful compared with other deserts.

THE CHIHUAHUAN DESERT ECOREGION

A GREAT MANY SPECIES of cactus thrive throughout this desert, though in the New Mexico portion of it more shrubs and native grasses will be seen than cacti or other plants. In fact, shrubs like Creosote Bush and mesquite define the Chihuahuan Desert in our state.

Such plants are called "indicator species" because their presence reflects the specific environmental conditions—soil, topography, and climate—required for them to grow in any particular place. Creosote Bush is the indicator for the outer limit of this desert in New Mexico. Driving south from Albuquerque on I-25, less than an hour after leaving the city and before passing through the town of Socorro, you will notice an abrupt change in roadside vegetation. Dark green scraggly-looking shrubs seem to be covering the landscape wherever you look. Ecologists consider the sudden appearance of Creosote Bush here to mark the northern limit of the Chihuahuan Desert ecoregion.

Separated by many miles from the true Chihuahuan Desert, several hillsides covered with Creosote Bush show up as islands of vegetation growing on black lava outcrops just south of Albuquerque. Look for these Creosote Bush islands on the right side of the interstate after crossing the Rio Grande. I first noticed some patches of this shrub here twenty-seven years ago, and I've

VEGETATION

Desert bloom along I-10, May 2010. Mexican Poppies are annual plants that bloom only for a week or two following spring rains. Mesquite and Soaptree Yucca are year-round residents. CCB

observed how the shrub has been expanding its territory over the years since then. I believe the shrub's northern march is just one more piece of evidence of global warming.

Creosote Bush

Creosote Bush is one of the best examples of a plant that has evolved to withstand harsh desert conditions. It competes aggressively with other plants for water and usually wins, since its massive root system is so efficient in absorbing moisture. The tiny waxy leaves then prevent excess loss of fluid during scorching summer heat.

Strangely, Creosote Bush originated as a species in South America, where it's still common in parts of the Andes. Then the plant slowly migrated north before the last ice age and finally reigned over the newly developing Chihuahuan Desert about five thousand years ago. One group of scientists believe that a single cluster of Creosote Bush in California may be the world's oldest living object. This particular plant—now somewhat famous—has been carbon-dated to 11,700 years old.

Island of Creosote Bush on I-25 south of Albuquerque. CCB

Creosote Bush, indicator plant of the Chihuahuan Desert. WWD

Mesquite

Another widespread plant here, mesquite, has an even more extensive range in New Mexico than Creosote Bush. It differs from most of the other Chihuahuan Desert shrubs in being deciduous—shedding its leaves in winter. Three species of mesquite grow here, but the one called Honey Mesquite prevails. All mesquites in America are armed with spines.

To many Americans, mesquite means wood chips and charcoal for a flavorful outdoor barbecue, or conjures up the image of a lonesome cowboy in the old days looking for a patch of desert shade. It may come as a surprise to learn that mesquite was the most important natural resource for many native peoples who lived in the American Southwest before the time of Columbus—people who utilized virtually every part of the plant. Not only were cooked mesquite beans a food staple but plant parts were also used for medicine, dye, cosmetics, shelter, tools, fiber, and fuel. As a matter of fact, for desert-dwelling people like the southern Apaches, mesquite was the staff of life.

Cacti Everywhere

To be sure, cacti are definitely the spiniest plants found here. Far more species grow in this desert than in the rest of the U.S. combined; in fact, it's believed that one-fifth of all the world's cacti occur in the Chihuahuan Desert, which certainly makes it a cactus lover's paradise. Most of them here are low-growing plants, inconspicuous unless they are blooming, but their stems can be in the shape of columns, balls, pads, or pencils. It's the stems that define them, for true cactus leaves are either greatly reduced or absent.

The Barrel Cactus, which may grow up to four feet tall, is our largest. At the other extreme, the ball-shaped Button Cactus is seldom much more

Honey Mesquite. WWD

Barrel Cactus. WWD

than an inch in diameter, and some of the well-named pincushion cacti aren't much bigger. Inch-wide stems on the Night-blooming Cereus can grow up to six feet long. Prickly Pears with their pad-like stems, are the most numerous, with more than a dozen species in southern New Mexico.

Don't look for towering Saguaro Cactus, our accustomed symbol for deserts everywhere, it seems. The Saguaro and other tall cacti grow only in the Sonoran Desert of southern Arizona and Mexico.

About the tallest spine-covered plant growing in southern New Mexico is the Ocotillo, which is not a cactus but a member of its own North American family of only eleven species. (By comparison, the Sunflower family has nearly twenty thousand.) For much of the year Ocotillos appear to be nothing more than an arrangement of ten- to twenty-foot-tall spiny dead sticks. With rainfall, the plants sprout clusters of tiny leaves on each stalk and bright crimson flowers at the tips.

Soaptree Yucca is another lofty plant that almost defines the Chihuahuan Desert. You won't mistake these desert wonders, since their huge rosettes of strap-like leaves atop stout trunks that can be more than twenty feet tall invariably give them away. Creamy white flowers on long stalks extend even farther skyward.

Desert Grasslands

Sweeping flats of grass where Creosote Bush and other shrubs are only widely scattered typify this desert. Grasslands develop where silt and clay soils retain more moisture than the usual coarse-textured rocky soils. They occur in areas of somewhat higher annual precipitation, such as elevated basins and north-facing slopes. Two hundred years ago the grasslands were more widespread here, but heavy grazing around the turn of the nineteenth century fragmented much of the grass cover, allowing shrubs to invade. Some areas are being converted to nearly pure

Ocotillo, the tallest of the spiny plants. WWD

Soaptree Yucca. WWD

shrublands as the grasses continue to decline due to erosion, drought, and climate change.

Otero Mesa between Alamogordo and the Texas border contains the largest expanse—nearly a million acres—of healthy native Black Grama grassland found anywhere. No paved roads penetrate the heart of this unique public grassland, but you will catch glimpses of it to the north when driving from El Paso to Carlsbad. Environmentalists are determined to prevent exploratory drilling for gas and oil here, concerned that the hundreds of miles of new roads, along with the pipelines, well pads, and waste pits that will be required, would forever alter and eventually destroy this national treasure.

Rare Plants

Rare plant species—often endangered plants—occur in microhabitats where soils or other environmental conditions are unique. Because of its many specialized soil types, the Chihuahuan Desert is host to dozens of rare plants, several of which are designated as endangered or threatened under the Federal Endangered Species Act. One of them, a plant called Feltleaf Bluestar, grows in a tiny patch not far from Carlsbad. When I discovered these few plants in 1990 while serving as a biologist for the Nature Conservancy, it was the first sighting in New Mexico—the only other one at that time being in Texas. Feltleaf Bluestar is definitely one of the rarest plants in the world.

Black Grama on Otero Mesa. WWD

A number of other extremely rare plants have found niches in some of the hard-to-reach canyons in the Guadalupe Mountains west of Carlsbad. Rare plants that are tucked away in limestone cracks and crevices in these mountains include species of columbine, milkwort, pennyroyal, and two different daisies.

COMPARED WITH NEW MEXICO'S MOUNTAINS or some of our grasslands, wildlife is less visible here just as it is in most other deserts. That's because so many of the desert animals are nocturnal or less active during the heat of the day. You may spot a coyote, jackrabbit, or ground squirrel, but casual travelers shouldn't expect to see many other mammals. However, a determined naturalist who is familiar with the habits of desert animals may come across a Collared Peccary, Spotted Ground Squirrel, Kit Fox, or even a Desert Bighorn Sheep.

Snakes and lizards thrive in our southern deserts, and several species are centered here that are not found elsewhere. The Collared Lizard is always a favorite due to its large size and striking collar. But don't attempt to capture one, for they tend to be pugnacious and most likely will try to bite. A number of the Chihuahuan Desert reptiles are restricted to sky island habitats.

More than four hundred and fifty species of birds have been recorded in the northern half of this desert; however, many are migratory and will be seen

ANIMAL LIFE

Feltleaf Bluestar —only a few populations occur in New Mexico and Texas. WWD

only during certain seasons. The grasslands here serve as important wintering grounds for a large proportion of the birds that spend their summers on the Great Plains. Sprague's Pipits, Chestnut-collared Longspurs, Grasshopper Sparrows, and Lark Buntings are among them.

One group of specialized mammals that make their home in the northern Chihuahuan Desert are bats. The best place to count on seeing great numbers of them is at Carlsbad Caverns National Park, where every evening in summer National Park Service naturalists conduct a bat-flight viewing program in the amphitheater at the entrance to the cave. The sight of thousands of Mexican Free-tailed Bats emerging from their daytime roosts down in the cave can be awesome.

Mexican Free-tailed Bats are one of the most abundant mammals in North America, and their roosting colonies comprise the largest congrega-

Collared Lizard on lava flow at the Valley of Fires Recreation Area. Photo: Mo O'Connor

Mexican Free-tailed Bats exiting from the mouth of Carlsbad Caverns. WWD

tions of mammals anywhere (apart from humans living in the world's largest cities). About four hundred thousand of them roost in the main cave at Carlsbad Caverns each summer. Consuming enormous quantities of moths and other insects, they are one of nature's most valuable pest predators, but poisoning from farm pesticides has been causing an alarming decline in their numbers. And a new threat to bats surfaced when a fungus that causes white-nose syndrome began killing bats at a fearful rate in the northeastern states in 2007. As of early 2011, it had not been detected in any New Mexico bat populations, but Carlsbad Caverns National Park has enacted a screening program to ensure that visitors are not bringing the fungus into the cave.

DESERT BIGHORN SHEEP

With their unique padded hooves, stocky Desert Bighorn Sheep are able to climb steep, rocky terrain with great agility. Desert Bighorns were common in the mountains of the Southwest until disease transmitted from domestic sheep reduced their numbers to just a few hundred in the mid-1900s, with very few scattered bands remaining in New Mexico's southern mountains. Under a State Game and Fish Department management program, the native sheep population has trended upward to the point where more than five hundred are believed to reside in the state today.

Desert Bighorn Sheep. Photo: Rachel L. Barr

MAGNIFICENT LANDFORMS

MUCH OF THE CHIHUAHUAN DESERT is underlain by limestone, although volcanic rocks and, occasionally, sandstone crop out in places. Limestone gives rise to soils that support unique plants—one of the reasons that vegetation in the Chihuahuan Desert is so diverse. Because limestone can be water soluble, nearly all of the world's largest caves are found in limestone country. Carlsbad Caverns is certainly one of the most famous and is a must-see for travelers to southern New Mexico. Altogether there are more than one hundred limestone caves within Carlsbad Caverns National Park.

This is a land of "sky-islands"—endless small, sparsely vegetated mountain ranges that rise up from the vast grass and shrub-covered flatlands. Streams and lakes are virtually nonexistent. Some of the ranges and desert basins have wonderful Anglo and Spanish names like Big Hatchet, Little Hatchet, Tres Hermanas (three sisters), Caballo (horse), and Jornada del Muerto (journey of death).

A few of New Mexico's Chihuahuan ranges are broader and support woodlands made up of junipers, Piñon Pines, and low-growing oaks. To get a taste of such woodlands, take the highway between Lordsburg and Silver City, which passes through the Burro Mountains, a small range underlaid by a core of granite rock.

Southwest of these mountains the Continental Divide zigzags along and between these ranges. East of Deming you can get out of your vehicle and straddle the divide on utterly flat ground where it crosses I-10 at an elevation of 4,585 feet. If you can locate the precise point, you can stand on the backbone of North America and put one foot on soil that drains to the Pacific Ocean and the other on land dipping off to the Atlantic.

Dry lake beds, known as playas, are a regular feature of this desert, and a good example of them can be seen a few miles west of Lordsburg. Here, the Lordsburg Playas on either side of the interstate provide a welcome break in the flat, shrubby landscape.

Limestone strata, typical of the Chihuahuan Desert, are exposed in a canyon below the highway from Cloudcroft to Alamogordo. CCB

Calcite crystals garnish the Bifrost Room, one of the most decorated areas in Carlsbad Caverns. Photo: National Park Service

Playas often occur where broad valleys have no drainage outlet. Because of constant evaporation, the centers of these shallow basins tend to be extremely alkaline and devoid of vegetation, with highly specialized salt-tolerant plants ringing the edges. In some years playas collect standing water for weeks or even months at a time during the wet season and so can be important stopovers for migrating shorebirds and waterfowl. The Lordsburg Playas are a remaining vestige of ancient Lake Animas, which was seventeen miles long and fifty feet deep during the last ice age twelve thousand years ago.

Driving south from Carlsbad you will come across some very unusual terrain—the Yeso Hills—just before crossing the New Mexico–Texas state line. Here the exposed bare land has a whitish cast, and the vegetation is remarkably different—all due to the presence of the mineral gypsum in the soil. Gyp soils, as they are called, are not uncommon in New Mexico, but where the mineral concentration is high, only certain plants can survive. Some of these gypsum-demanding species, including one whose scientific name is *Anulocaulis gypsogenus*, grow nowhere else. Another is a wild buckwheat named *Eriogonum gypsophilum* that is found only in this vicinity and is so rare that it has been designated a threatened species by the Federal Endangered Species Act. It's worth stopping in the Yeso Hills and walking around to take in some of the strange plant life.

The Tres Hermanas Mountains south of Deming are typical of the many "sky island" ranges along I-10. WWD

I-10 crosses a low point on the Continental Divide. CCB

The Lordsburg Playas are typical of these common features of the Chihuahuan Desert. CCB

White Sands National Monument

Because gypsum can dissolve in water over time, the mineral is rarely found in the form of sand. But conditions in the Tularosa Basin west of Alamogordo have resulted in the creation of the world's largest gypsum dune fields. These dunes are now preserved in one of our state's best-loved national monuments— White Sands.

The glistening pure white dunes that have engulfed 275 square miles of the Tularosa Basin are geologically very young, having been deposited since the last ice age as recently as 6,500 years ago. Today the dunes are constantly changing shape and slowly moving downwind. The few plant species that populate the dunes must be able to grow rapidly enough to avoid being buried in the shifting sands. Several species of small animals—a mouse, two lizards, and several insects—have evolved a pale coloration that camouflages them in the gypsum sand. Viewing is best in the early morning and evening when low light brings out shadows and the subtle colors of the dunes.

A Recent Volcano

Evidence of ancient volcanoes can be seen in all of New Mexico's major ecoregions, and the Chihuahuan Desert is no exception. A lava flow known as the Carrizozo Malpais (badlands) is the most spectacular volcanic feature in the southern half of our state. Less than one thousand years ago lava poured forth from a small volcano north of what is now the town of Carrizozo and flowed south down a stream valley in the

Soaptree Yucca thrives on gyp soils in the Yeso Hills south of Carlsbad. WWD

Anulocaulis gypsogenus, a gypsophile plant, grows in the Yeso Hills. WWD

Eriogonum gypsophilum, another gypsum-demanding species. WWD

The pink plant is Sand Verbena; the yucca is Soaptree Yucca. CCB

Tularosa Basin nearly to where the dunes of White Sands begin to take shape. You can walk right onto the black lava formations at the Valley of Fires Recreation Area four miles west of Carrizozo.

You might think that this thick lava flow wouldn't support much life, but you'd be wrong. In fact, the Carrizozo Malpais is remarkable in its support of a high diversity of plant species, one hundred and forty of which have been identified here. This is in contrast to the much lower number of species growing on the adjacent flats and is due to the greater availability of moisture on the flow resulting from protected sinkholes and crevices that effectively retain soil and water.

Despite its young age, evolutionary genetics is already under way here in the form of adaptive coloration. Several species of rodents living on the flow are considerably darker than the same critters living off it. The coloration contrast is particularly striking for identical species that also inhabit White Sands not many miles to the south, where their pelage is much paler.

WATER IN THE DESERT

WATER IS THE GREAT SUSTAINER OF LIFE in all deserts, and the Chihuahuan is no exception. July and August, when monsoon moisture sweeps in from the Gulf of Mexico, are the wettest months, and this mid-summer moisture can prolong a wildflower show that normally begins in late April. However, many native plants, such as Mexican Poppies, are annuals and won't be seen blooming in those years when spring rains are meager.

Many animals and most riparian plants need a year-round source of water—which can be from rivers, intermittent streams, ponds, springs, or seeps. Reptiles and a few mammals like Kangaroo Rats can live their lives without a drink of free water. They simply derive their moisture by metabolic means or from succulent vegetation.

Only three real rivers flow through the Chihuahuan Desert in our state. The Rio Grande, typically lined with cottonwoods and Tamarisk, known in the west as Salt Cedar, courses down through the center of this ecoregion as it

The thousand-year-old lava flow at the Valley of Fires is already plant-covered. At 12,003 feet, Sierra Blanca dominates the skyline. CCB

makes its way to the Gulf of Mexico in south Texas. The Pecos River, originating in the mountains east of Santa Fe, runs through the city of Carlsbad and flows into the Rio Grande more than two hundred miles downstream. The Pecos is not always free-flowing, however. I can recall an attempt to canoe a stretch of it south of Carlsbad when the venture involved far more portaging than paddling.

At the point where it flows out of the mountains, the Gila River—the third major river in our part of the Chihuahuan Desert—marks the northwest edge of the desert. Instead of pure stands of cottonwoods, so typical of other riverbanks elsewhere in New Mexico, Arizona Sycamores are the dominant tree along this river's edge. These magnificent trees with their puzzle-like whitish bark barely spill into New Mexico from their native habitat in southeastern Arizona.

Pecos River east of Roswell. WWD

Gila River above Gila. CCB

Standing water or water dripping out from seeps or springs is a magnet for desert birds and other wildlife, and specialized riparian vegetation is a hallmark of these green oases. The best-known Chihuahuan Desert spring in New Mexico, one that is easily accessible to the public, is Rattlesnake Springs adjacent to Carlsbad Caverns National Park. It's an open pool nourished by water welling up from below that feeds into a quarter-mile-long wetland where sedges and cattails flourish under majestic cottonwoods. Rattlesnake Springs attracts migrating birds, including some colorful rarely seen species such as the Painted Bunting and Vermilion Flycatcher. More than three hundred other birds have been recorded here, along with an unusual number of rare amphibians, reptiles, and butterflies.

(opposite)
Vermilion Flycatcher. Photo:
Scott Streit

Snow Geese at Bosque del
Apache, February 24, 2011.
WWD

Rattlesnake Springs. CCB

EL CAMINO REAL
NATIONAL SCENIC BYWAY

WHEN DON JUAN OÑATE led five hundred soldiers and prospective colonists who were driving some seven thousand head of livestock from inland Mexico to northern New Mexico in 1598, the Southwest and its people were changed forever. Once Oñate's wagon train reached present-day El Paso on that historic seven-hundred-mile journey, the expedition followed the Rio Grande Valley upriver all the way to the place where the Rio Grande intersects the Chama River, some thirty miles north of Santa Fe. Their livestock were the first large domestic animals to enter our state, and livestock ended up having a huge impact on both the native people and the land itself.

In the centuries following the establishment of the American Southwest's original Spanish colony, this route became the primary north-south road linking New Mexico to Mexico City. It was soon being called El Camino Real de Tierra Adentro (The King's Highway to the Interior Lands). In fact, Las Cruces (the crosses) is thought to have been named for the crosses on graves of early unfortunate Spanish travelers on El Camino Real.

Interstate 25 closely parallels that route today, and from Santa Fe to the Mexican border it has been designated as El Camino Real National Scenic Byway. Although human history is the focus of this scenic byway, its natural scenery is wonderfully varied. As I-25 makes its way through two of New Mexico's major ecoregions—the Great Basin Grassland and the Chihuahuan Desert— travelers will note a dramatic change in roadside vegetation from juniper-covered grasslands in the north to Creosote Bush–dominated hills and flats down south.

Without a doubt, the best-known natural landmark just off this route is Bosque del Apache National Wildlife Refuge located a few miles south of Socorro. Six square miles of old irrigated farms and wetlands comprise the heart of this refuge, while arid grasslands and Chihuahuan shrublands surround the core. A twelve-mile loop road takes visitors by many ponds and canals where waterfowl and shorebirds are plentiful year-round. The greatest number of birds are seen from late November through late February when as many as ten thousand Sand Hill Cranes and twenty thousand dazzling white Ross's and Snow Geese make the refuge their winter home. Every year in November the weeklong Festival of the Cranes draws thousands from all over the world to hear lectures, attend workshops, and, of course, see the bird display. Bird diversity peaks again in late April and early May. A desert botanical garden where travelers can get to know some key Chihuahuan plants is maintained next to the refuge visitor center.

A little farther south, El Camino Real International Heritage Center is the place to learn about this historic route. Opened to the public in 2005, the center contains award-winning exhibits and original artifacts that interpret the role of our nation's oldest continuously used highway. It tells the story of three centuries of trade, commerce, conflict, and the eventual confluence of cultures linking Spain, Mexico, and the United States.

One of the dozens of ponds at Bosque del Apache National Wildlife Refuge. CCB

2 GREAT BASIN DESERT

FIRST
IMPRESSIONS

WHETHER APPROACHING THE FOUR CORNERS from Albuquerque heading to Farmington or from I-40 through Gallup or Crownpoint, you are bound to be struck by the variety and grandeur of this land's rock formations. So much bare earth and rock is exposed here—a lot of it spectacularly rugged and almost always colorful. A large part of the Great Basin Desert is badlands country, and that's particularly true for the New Mexico portion of it.

Apart from dramatic rock formations and brightly tinted soils, some people find these landscapes a bit monotonous. The corridor along the San Juan River is well wooded, but elsewhere about the only trees in the desert proper are junipers, and many of them aren't much larger than oversize shrubs. Gray-green tones characterize a good deal of the vegetation, for this desert is dominated by sagebrush, while grasses and other vegetation tend to be sparse at best.

Being a desert, of course it's hot in summer but usually not unbearably so. On the other hand, temperatures well below freezing coupled with blowing snow can greet the traveler on any given day in winter.

Farmington is New Mexico's only real city to have been settled in the Great Basin Desert.

(previous)
Bisti Badlands. CCB

*Badlands in the Great Basin Desert
ecoregion, with Shiprock in the distance. CCB*

*Iron-rich soils provide many shades of red
across the badlands. CCB*

GREAT BASIN DESERT ECOREGION

DESERTS ARE RECENT FEATURES of the American landscape. In fact, true deserts didn't exist here twelve thousand years ago, and they may have evolved as recently as in the past five thousand years. The Great Basin Desert is the most northerly of the four deserts in North America. The other three, the Mojave, Sonoran, and Chihuahuan Deserts, lie well to the south and are characterized by their much hotter climate.

This desert certainly is dry, with precipitation around the Four Corners averaging about eight inches per year, making it the driest place in our state year in and year out. Storms rolling inland from the Pacific are drained of moisture by the Sierra Nevada Mountains far to the west, which accounts for the dry conditions throughout the Great Basin. Compared with the other three, the Great Basin Desert is exceptionally cold in winter when maximum daily temperatures may remain well below freezing for days on end from December through February. High elevation partly accounts for the cool climate; the Four Corners region is about the same elevation as Denver—roughly a mile high.

Technically, the Great Basin, a geographic province that covers most of Nevada and parts of eastern California, southeastern Oregon, southern Idaho, and eastern Utah, doesn't quite extend into New Mexico. That's because by definition this geographical province is a completely closed basin with no river outlet to the ocean. For that reason a number of salty lakes, such as the Great Salt Lake in Utah, along with many playas have formed throughout the basin proper. However, from an ecological perspective, taking into account native plant and animal life, a slice of the Great Basin Desert does protrude into New Mexico, but just barely. This desert is the smallest major ecoregion in our state, with the greater part of it on Navajo Indian Reservation land.

VEGETATION

VARIOUS KINDS OF SPINELESS SHRUBS make up the vegetation here, with Big Sagebrush being the dominant plant throughout the desert. Piñon Pines and Utah Junipers are scattered across the land in places where a little extra moisture can be tapped, but because of the extremely cold winters, relatively few species of cactus occur in the Great Basin Desert. Those that do grow here tend to have short stature, for example the ground-hugging varieties of Prickly Pear or Claret-cup. About the only tall cacti are chollas with their thin cylindrical stems and magenta blossoms.

A century or so ago this land would have appeared quite a bit more lush, with good stands of grasses growing between patches of shrubs. But grazing began to take a toll, and when it peaked around the turn of the nineteenth century, enormous numbers of sheep and cattle were pounding away at the vegetation year after year. Many of the perennial grasses like Indian Ricegrass are nearly gone, replaced in part by introduced annual grasses such as

The Great Basin Desert is a sagebrush-dominated ecoregion. CCB

Big Sagebrush. WWD

Cheatgrass, an alien that out-competes native grasses. As a result of past over-grazing, Big Sagebrush has increased dramatically over the past hundred years.

Vast stands of pale-gray turquoise color announce the presence of this shrub—probably the most common plant in the western states. Even from a distance Big Sagebrush will be recognized by its smoky color and uniform spacing of plants. On closer examination its strong turpentine fragrance, especially after a rainstorm, is a dead giveaway. Pinch a few three-toothed leaves to get the effect.

Long ago the Fremont people who lived northwest of the Four Corners had developed an industry where most everything that was woven or crafted from plant material was made from Big Sagebrush. In more recent times Indians from many different tribes have collected plant parts for medicinal and ceremonial purposes. The leaves are still used to combat digestive problems, headaches, and colds, and as a general stimulant by the Hopi, who regard Big Sagebrush as being more potent than related species of sagebrush that grow on their reservation.

The Navajo boil an extract of leaves for coughs, colds, headaches, stomachaches, and fevers, as well as for pain during child delivery. It's one of the Navajo "life medicines" and may be the wild plant most revered by these people. Navajo weavers also boil the leaves and twigs to produce various shades of yellow and gold dye for coloring their traditional blankets and rugs.

SPARSE ANIMAL LIFE

EXCEPT FOR SELDOM SEEN COYOTES, desert cottontails, jackrabbits, and pronghorn, mammal life in the Great Basin Desert is largely nocturnal. Kangaroo rats, pocket gophers, and pocket mice are among the nighttime denizens.

Because of the long, cold winters, not nearly as many reptiles live on the rocks and in the sand here as do in our warmer southern deserts. One of the most bizarre, the Desert Horned Lizard, looks like a miniature holdover from the dinosaur era. This spiny lizard burrows into the sand for cover, but if it becomes excited while on the surface, it puffs itself with air, making it look formidable. Horned lizards prey on ants and other insects.

As for birds, Golden Eagles seem to be more prevalent in the Great Basin than anywhere else in the U.S. Songbirds that flit about the sage-brush include the somewhat secretive Sage Sparrow and the robin-size Sage Thrasher, a bird noted for its rich, mockingbird-like song.

Desert Horned Lizard. Photo: Ron Wolf

Sage Sparrow. Photo: Scott Streit

SPECTACULAR GEOLOGY

OF THE MANY ROCK FORMATIONS and other scenic landforms in New Mexico, Shiprock, thirty miles west of Farmington, is surely the most awe-inspiring. Rising more than 1,600 feet above the surrounding desert, this formation is a classic textbook example of a volcanic plug that formed when molten lava solidified in the throat of an ancient volcano. Shiprock is in the heart of the Navajo Indian Reservation and has great religious and historical significance for all Navajos. Thus, climbing on the rock is forbidden by the tribe today.

Though not nearly so spectacular, a formation known as The Hogback cuts across the highway between Shiprock and Farmington. The Hogback is a steeply uptilted band of sandstone that runs for miles to the north and south. The northern end is noted for being a critical habitat for a number of rare plant species, including the officially endangered Mancos Milkvetch, a low-growing legume with bright magenta flowers.

The Chuska Mountains are the only significant range in the New Mexico portion of the Great Basin Desert. Running north and south along the Arizona border, these mountains were the source of timbers that were hauled to Chaco Canyon and used to make roof support beams for the multistory urban complexes constructed by ancestral Puebloans more than a thousand years ago. Some forty-five thousand pine, spruce, and fir logs were needed to complete the largest structures at Chaco. Lacking domestic livestock of any kind, the Chacoans carried the logs on their backs up to a distance of fifty miles—an astonishing feat of endurance. Livestock that could have been used for transport didn't arrive in the New World until Columbus brought a menagerie on his second voyage in 1493, so all work had to be done by humans in those days.

Without a doubt, the most bizarre set of landforms in this desert is found in the Bisti Badlands, an amazing expanse of undulating mounds and peculiarly eroded rock formations that are colored by a vivid mix of red, gray, orange, or brown tints. These strange badlands are within the forty-five-thousand-acre De-Na-Zin Bisti Wilderness Area thirty-five miles due south of Farmington. Short trails lead out into this completely barren landscape, allowing you a close look at the hoodoos, balanced rocks, and small slot canyons—all carved by wind and water.

(top)
The Hogback, an uplift formation of sandstone strata, runs for miles west of Farmington. CCB

(above and left)
The Bisti Badlands is a colorful expanse of steeply eroded rock formations south of Farmington. CCB

Webster's defines badlands as "a region marked by intricate erosional sculpturing, scanty vegetation, and fantastically formed hills," and New Mexico certainly has its share of them. Water constantly erodes the typically soft rock formations, and daytime meltwater from snow in winter freezes at night, splitting open the vertical cracks and accelerating erosion even more.

Such continuous erosion doesn't allow many plants to get a toehold on the rock faces, yet some plant life does manage to survive there. Colorful, crusty lichens—actually microscopic fungi and algae growing symbiotically—colonize some of the more protected rock surfaces, and mosses find a niche in shady cracks.

Contrast this arid scene with how New Mexico's environment would have looked ten thousand years ago, when the climate was much cooler and wetter. In those days the land was covered with conifers and deciduous woodlands interspersed with shrubs and savannas of tallgrass prairie. Huge mammals, including herding beasts such as mammoths, horses, and camels, as well as ground sloths, giant armadillos, saber-toothed cats, and oversize bears roamed across the landscape. But all of them disappeared with the warming and drying of our climate.

HOME TO PREHISTORIC PUEBLOANS AND MODERN NAVAJOS

EVEN AS RECENTLY AS A THOUSAND YEARS AGO the Four Corners region was somewhat wetter than today. Water flowed down Chaco Wash then, and New Mexico's most advanced prehistoric culture flourished in Chaco Canyon. An estimated five thousand residents lived in apartment-like adobe complexes up to five stories tall. They basically were urban farmers who cultivated corn, beans, and squash in terraced gardens, oversaw a system of some four

Painted Desert in the Bisti Badlands. CCB

hundred miles of trade-route roadways, and made astronomical calculations to properly align their many structures. Despite such progress, when drought struck the region in 1090 followed by a prolonged period of little rain in the next century, Chaco was abandoned, and the people built new pueblos along the Rio Grande and other places where they could find water. Chaco is a National Historic Park and a UNESCO World Heritage Site today—a must-visit for anyone with a keen interest in southwestern archaeology.

During the century before the Spaniards colonized New Mexico, nomadic Navajo Indians moved into the Four Corners region and soon took to growing corn. Eventually they acquired Spanish sheep, embracing a pastoral life that continues for many of them. Today Navajo weavers convert sheep wool into magnificent rugs and blankets, and other artisans craft elegant jewelry, making the Navajo Indian Reservation one more reason to spend some time in this corner of the state.

SO LITTLE WATER

DRY WASHES AND ARROYOS abound in this desert. After a heavy summer thundershower, they can become temporary raging torrents and therefore a potential danger to backcountry motorists, but ninety-nine percent of the time they are bone-dry. Nevertheless, residual underground moisture may support some semi-riparian vegetation such as introduced Salt Cedars or native Rubber Rabbitbrush, more commonly known as Chamisa.

The San Juan River is the only consistently flowing water in the region. It's a four-hundred-mile-long major tributary of the Colorado River that drains much of the arid land west of the Southern Rockies before it courses through the Grand Canyon. Like most of the true rivers in New Mexico, majestic cottonwoods and willows along with introduced Salt Cedar line its banks. Just below Navajo Dam a few miles upstream from where it enters the Great Basin Desert, the San Juan is known as one of the premier fly-fishing waters in the nation. This river truly beautifies the city of Farmington as it splits the town down the middle.

Pueblo Bonito, a five-story-tall pueblo at Chaco Culture National Historical Park. WWD

Russian Olive trees line the banks of the San Juan River west of Farmington. CCB

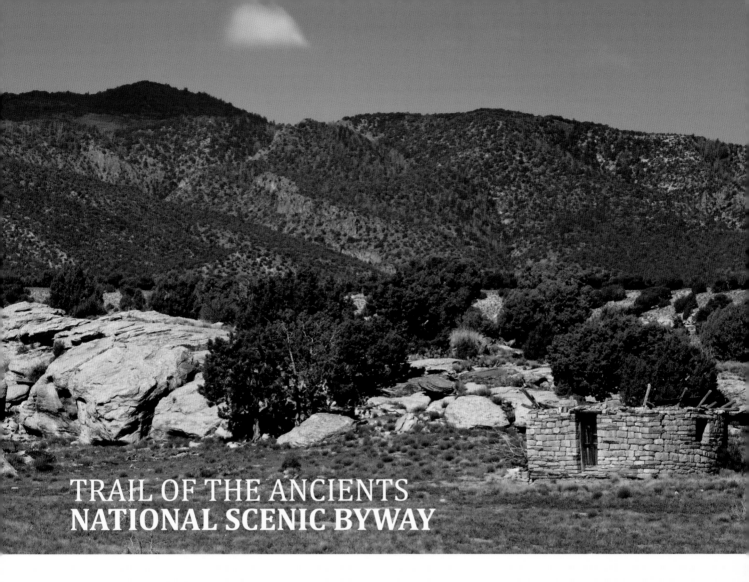

TRAIL OF THE ANCIENTS
NATIONAL SCENIC BYWAY

THIS SCENIC BYWAY is a network of virtually all the paved roads and some of the unpaved ones that crisscross the Great Basin Desert ecoregion, so it's not a route that makes a loop or beckons to be driven in its entirety, unless you are a true desert rat. Besides passing by some of the most prominent geological formations in this high desert, it leads to many of New Mexico's top archaeological sites. The wealth of these attractions includes, first and foremost, Chaco Culture National Historical Park, along with Aztec Ruins National Monument and Salmon Ruins and Heritage Park. The Bisti Wilderness Area and Angel Peak National Recreation Area along with Shiprock itself, the beacon of this desert, are fantastic geological points of interest.

Most of the trail-road is on Navajo land, and traveling the route can be a great introduction to Navajo culture. Toadlena and Two Grey Hills are classic old trading posts that display Navajo rug weaving at its finest. The latter, which boasts an original stone-and-adobe store, is one of the few remaining historic posts on the Navajo Indian Reservation. The tiny village of Crownpoint has built a reputation for its monthly auction of Navajo rugs from area weavers. Of course, Navajo jewelry and pottery are also available for purchase at these and many other sites along the Trail of the Ancients.

Navajo hogan at the base of the Chuska Mountains. CCB

3 GREAT BASIN GRASSLAND

FIRST
IMPRESSIONS

OF ALL NEW MEXICO'S major ecoregions, the Great Basin Grassland is the least distinctive. No single plant like Creosote Bush in the Chihuahuan Desert or Big Sagebrush in the Great Basin Desert dominates this ecoregion. Along with our deserts, this ecoregion tends to be somewhat shrubby, particularly where heavy sheep and cattle grazing in the past has led to the encroachment of Broom Snakeweed, Cane Cholla, and low-growing junipers. Though ecologists label this a grassland, pure stands of grass are hard to find today. Color this land brown in fall, winter, and early spring, but when monsoon rains arrive in June or July during most years, the entire countryside springs to life. May is usually the month for the best wildflower show.

More than half of New Mexico's population resides in or on the edge of this ecoregion, which encompasses major cities like Albuquerque, Rio Rancho, and Santa Fe. That's due more to the early Spanish colonists choosing to settle along the Rio Grande than to the nature of the land itself. Soils in the valley are some of the best in the state, leading to modest agricultural enterprise on either side of I-25.

Low hills, mesas, or mountains are almost always within view, and this region has more than its share of spectacular volcanic rock formations.

(previous)
Approaching storm. CCB

NEW MEXICO'S GRASSLANDS

GRASSLANDS—areas where the vegetation is dominated by native species of grass—have developed everywhere in the world in regions with rainfall averaging between ten and thirty-five inches per year. Because of their massive root systems and their relatively small leaf surfaces, most native grasses are able to cope with drought. A grass that is barely a few inches tall may have a four-foot long root system. Grasses are able to close the tiny pores in their leaves that would allow evaporation and to curl their leaves to further reduce water loss.

Grasslands are the most extensive vegetation community in New Mexico, covering more than a third of the state. They have evolved here over the millennia at elevations between four and seven thousand feet where annual moisture is in the ten- to twenty-inch range. Smaller meadows are found at higher elevations, where the grass benefits from cooler temperatures and much higher precipitation. Nearly all of our lower-elevation grasslands are bordered by juniper or Piñon-Juniper Woodlands wherever the terrain rises toward hills, mesas, or mountains.

Most of New Mexico's grasslands are dotted with all kinds of shrubs and small trees. But up until the middle to late 1800s, these grasslands contained far fewer woody plants than they do today. Early Anglo explorers told of vast expanses of nearly pure grass. One traveler wrote of "hundreds and hundreds of thousands of acres, containing the greatest abundance of the finest grass in the world."

Human activities have been the agents of change over the past century. Farming, livestock ranching, fire suppression, and water diversion have reduced both the size and the quality of our grasslands, allowing shrubby plants to invade. The future of New Mexico's grasslands depends upon land stewardship—whether willy-nilly or wise.

Shrubs and small junipers typically thrive among the grasses in the Great Basin Grassland ecoregion. WWD

New Mexico's grasses can be grouped into two types—cool-season and warm-season. Cool-season grasses start their growth early in the spring and continue growing for as long as rain and cool temperatures prevail. Grassy slopes and flats that have greened up in May or June are covered with cool-season grasses. Indian Ricegrass and New Mexico Feathergrass are among the commonest in the Great Basin Grassland.

Up to two feet tall and having bell-shaped papery bracts that encase each plump seed, Indian Ricegrass is one of the easiest grasses to identify. It was surely the most valuable wild cereal harvested by Pueblo Indians during prehistoric times. Being a cool-season grass, its seeds could be gathered months before their fields of cultivated corn were ready to be harvested. The grains would have been tossed in a basket with hot coals, then ground up to concoct a healthy gruel. Rodents commonly cache the seeds underground, allowing Indian Ricegrass to spread to new locations.

Wherever you spot silvery waves of tall grass growing on gentle slopes in central New Mexico during late May or early June, it's likely to be our most beautiful grass, New Mexico Feathergrass, blowing in the wind. Both Indian Ricegrass and this species thrive on sandy soils where spring moisture has penetrated deeply.

Our warm-season grasses don't green up until midsummer. Because of their extensive root systems, they are conservators of water and nutrients. Low water requirements allow these grasses to remain green and growing even after the monsoon rains of July and August have ceased. The most common species across the state are the various grama grasses—Blue Grama in the northern two-thirds of the state and Black Grama in the south.

The Impact of Grazing

Except for llamas in the South American Andes, large domesticated animals were absent from the New World until they arrived with Columbus. Accompanying the Spaniards were horses, cattle, sheep, goats, and pigs that spread across the continent, reaching New Mexico in 1598 with the arrival of Juan de Oñate and his throng of colonizers. Livestock numbers slowly increased as new colonies became established, but during the first two and a half centuries of Spanish and, later, Mexican rule, the imported animals had little impact upon the land itself.

However, by the 1870s heavy grazing was resulting in stream gullying and soil erosion, which allowed shrubs and

Indian Ricegrass. WWD

In late spring New Mexico Feathergrass waves in the wind. WWD

The presence of Cane Cholla and Broom Snakeweed on grasslands indicates a history of overgrazing. WWD

weeds to invade. By the turn of the century some five million sheep owned by Anglo and Hispanic ranchers were overgrazing New Mexico Territory, and it was sheep, not cattle, that were the principal culprits of grassland deterioration. Although livestock numbers have been greatly reduced since that time, and sheep and goat grazing is no longer much of an issue, the long-term effects of overgrazing aren't easily reversed. If you are interested in New Mexico's livestock story, you may wish to read my book *New Mexico's Spanish Livestock Heritage* (2012).

A Myriad of Plant Life

Though shrubs are scattered throughout the Great Basin Grassland ecoregion, no particular species is dominant. Arroyos—those water-carved gullies that run only after a heavy rain—are plentiful and are usually lined with shrubs or small trees that require a little extra moisture. Desert Willow, a small tree with striking orchid-shaped pink-and-white blossoms, and Apache Plume, whose white flowers turn into feathery pink seed plumes, are two of the most striking.

Several kinds of yucca crop up throughout these grasslands. Narrowleaf Yucca with its bladelike sharp-tipped leaves barely an inch wide frequently occurs on grassy flats, while Banana Yucca with thicker succulent leaves thrives in more rocky places. Both bear creamy white flowers on a single erect stalk, and the leaves of both are strengthened by long, tough fibers. Owing to these fibers and other attributes, yuccas were the single most important group of wild plants for prehistoric Indians living in the Southwest.

The thick, sweet fruit of Banana Yuccas formed a staple of prehistoric diets throughout the region. The "bananas" would have been eaten green or dried and stored for winter use.

Fiber from the leaves played an even more important role in the people's lives. In fact, throughout the Southwest no material was in greater demand for manufacturing cordage than yucca-leaf fiber. The long straight leaves would be soaked, then pounded with stones to extract the fibers that were then twisted to fabricate string or rope for lashing house beams, fixing ladder rungs, and making bowstrings and nets. Among other uses, virtually all sandals were made from yucca leaves as were many mats and baskets.

For ages an extract made from saponin-rich yucca roots was the equivalent of soap for most Indians living in the Southwest. Today the roots are still regularly sought by Pueblo Indians for concocting a shampoo. I've been told by male ceremonial dancers that a yucca shampoo makes their long hair shinier and blacker.

Yucca fibers were used by women at many of the Rio Grande pueblos to make brushes for rendering designs on their pottery. A leaf was chewed until the tip was finely frayed then the fringe employed as a paintbrush. Today

a number of Pueblo artists, notably several at Acoma Pueblo, still use a traditional Narrowleaf Yucca brush in decorating their beautiful handcrafted pots.

Brilliant Colors in the Fall

Golden borders along our roads in early fall signal the blooming of Rubber Rabbitbrush, or Chamisa, as this tall shrub is called in most parts of our state. Its affinity to roadsides is due to rabbitbrush needing more moisture than other shrubs common to the region, a requirement that is satisfied by additional runoff from highways during summer storms, which effectively doubles annual precipitation absorbed by soil along the road. Out in the grasslands proper Broom Snakeweed provides the golden hues. When Purple Aster with its royal-purple blossoms is mixed in with these golden-flowered shrubs, our northern highways can, indeed, become royal roads.

The most striking golden vistas in fall, however, owe their beauty to two native trees—Fremont Cottonwood along our watercourses and Quaking Aspen up in the mountains. For about three weeks in October or early November, a time when storms are rare and the air is crisp, driving in New Mexico becomes a truly dazzling experience.

BIRDLIFE IN THIS ECOREGION is particularly varied and plentiful, and the Roadrunner is hands down the public's favorite. This goofy-looking long-legged ground bird about the size of a chicken and capable of flight always draws a smile whenever it scoots across a highway. Roadrunners can run at speeds of up to twenty miles per hour in pursuit of grasshoppers, snakes, or

Apache Plume. WWD

Banana Yucca. WWD

Narrowleaf Yucca was a principal source of fibers for making cordage in prehistoric times. WWD

BIRDS AND MAMMALS

Rubber Rabbitbrush (also known as Chamisa). WWD

Purple Aster and golden composites create royal roads in the fall. WWD

Fremont Cottonwood. WWD

other small reptiles. They whack a snake or lizard with their beaks, then slam the victim against the ground for as long as it takes to kill the stunned prey. No wonder the Roadrunner has been designated the state bird of New Mexico.

Beyond an occasional Rock Squirrel, cottontail, and ubiquitous domestic livestock, the Great Basin Grassland ecoregion might strike you as being somewhat devoid of mammal life. And, except for nocturnal rodents, it generally is. Of the larger wild animals, coyotes are the most likely to be seen in daylight—trotting across a field singly or in pairs. Coyotes are smart and adaptable and have learned to live not just in the wild but at the edge of rural communities where they may raid gardens or garbage and hunt whatever is easiest to catch (including small pets). Where I live in Placitas, a rural village just north of Albuquerque, folks consider it a treat to hear a chorus of coyotes yipping their high-pitched song at night or in the early-morning hours. Coyotes are believed to be more numerous in New Mexico today than in prehistoric times, probably because of their inherited adaptability to changing conditions.

NEW MEXICO HAS MORE VOLCANOES and displays a greater range of past volcanic activity than anywhere else in the United States. Many of our most distinctive landscapes spotlight volcanoes and volcanic rocks. That's especially true of the Great Basin Grasslands, though there is little connection between past volcanism and what grows in this ecoregion today.

VOLCANOES AND OTHER LANDFORMS

This Roadrunner has captured a lizard.
Photo: Pat Gaines

More volcanoes can be seen from Albuquerque than from almost any other city in the world. Five of them are lined up just west of the city within Petroglyph National Monument. Seventy miles to the west, just north of I-40, Mount Taylor was active off and on two to four million years ago with eruptions similar to the 1980 eruption of Mount Saint Helens in Washington State. Mount Taylor can be seen from the city because of its high elevation—over 11,000 feet. Just north of Bernalillo on the west side of the Rio Grande the remains of several more small volcanoes jut above the land surface, and off in the distance the columnar basalt of Cabezon Peak rises nearly 2,000 feet

Mount Taylor is one of the many volcanoes that can be seen from Albuquerque. CCB

above the surrounding plain. But the mightiest of all is Jemez Volcano, visible on the far northern skyline. This million-year-old giant shaped much of the landscape west of Santa Fe and will be discussed in a later chapter. Nearly all volcanoes in central New Mexico are features associated with the great Rio Grande Rift that splits the state from north to south.

The Rio Grande Rift is a massive fracture in the earth's surface that began to form thirty million years ago and now extends from southern Colorado to El Paso, Texas. Geologic faults along this rift are pipelines for rising heat from the earth's interior—conduits that have allowed molten rock to reach the surface and produce the Albuquerque volcanoes.

The New Mexico portion of the rift created a shallow trench east of the Continental Divide through which the Rio Grande now flows. Whereas in most cases valleys are cut by rivers, the Rio Grande is doing its level best to fill the rift with sediment. The rift remains active today, and movement along its geological faults accounts for the minor earthquakes that periodically occur.

West of Albuquerque I-40 cuts through the northern tip of New Mexico's largest lava flow, named El Malpais by the early explorers because of the impossibility of moving their livestock across the land. The rumpled-looking shiny black lava seen here has resulted from the output of a number of small volcanoes that began discharging some eight hundred thousand years ago and have continued until the most recent eruption about three thousand years ago. The basalt flows filled a large natural basin that is rimmed by higher sandstone bluffs.

Some of this sandstone has been eroded by wind and water to produce fantastic shapes, including majestic La Ventana Natural Arch—the second largest in the state— on the east side of the flows. All features here are protected within El Malpais National Monument and El Malpais National Recreation Area, though some of the flows do extend onto private lands.

Curiously, the vegetation on this lava flow is utterly different from what grows on the state's other major flow—the Carrizozo Malpais at the foot of the Sacramento Mountains. In fact, only eighteen species of plants are common to both flows. Some of the oldest Douglas-firs on the planet have survived on the Malpais, and stands of Quaking Aspen have gotten a foothold in at least one place—well below the usual elevation for these trees. Part of the reason is that the lava substrate has the capacity to trap and retain moisture, allowing such trees to survive. It can be cold here, and permanent ice has accumulated in one collapsed lava tube where the temperature never rises above thirty-one degrees.

You can make a half-day drive that loops around the flows and goes by El Morro National Monument, where New Mexico's original Spanish colonist, Juan de Oñate,

La Ventana Natural Arch, the second largest in the state. CCB

Quaking Aspen growing on a lava flow at El Malpais. WWD

inscribed his name on a rock face in 1605. This 170-mile loop that traverses so much exciting scenery is not a designated scenic byway, but it should be.

New Mexico's Closed Basins

Not all flowing waters eventually empty into the sea. Many drain into closed basins that have no outlet, and our state has its share of them. The largest is the Tularosa Basin west of Alamogordo that covers 6,500 square miles. Others include Jornada del Muerto east of the Rio Grande (3,344 square miles), Salt Basin that projects up into the state from Texas (2,400 square miles in the New Mexico portion of it), and the Plains of San Agustin.

These plains, consisting of a flat grassland occupying nearly two thousand square miles west of Socorro, are surrounded by mountain ranges and are what remains of an ancient Pleistocene lake bed. The level ground here is the site of the Very Large Array—a collection of twenty-seven giant para-

PETROGLYPHS

In New Mexico black volcanic rock was definitely preferred by prehistoric Indians as the medium for pecking out the figures of people, animals, and mysterious objects on stone. These people had discovered that chipping away the rock's thin desert varnish revealed a lighter gray beneath and left a lasting mark.

A huge assortment of petroglyphs can be seen at two different public locations, each of them with more than twenty thousand images. The Three Rivers Petroglyph Site is not far from the Valley of Fires Recreation Area (described in chapter one). Petroglyph National Monument just west of Albuquerque is the other. Both sites offer trails where you can examine the inscriptions firsthand.

More than twenty thousand images have been recorded at the Three Rivers Petroglyph Site. WWD

bolic antennas arranged on railroad tracks in a Y shape. This mammoth radio observatory is designed to investigate distant astronomical objects, including galaxies, black holes, and radio-emitting stars. Contrary to pop culture, however, it has never been used to search for extraterrestrials.

EAST OF THE CONTINENTAL DIVIDE the Rio Grande (big river) flows from its headwaters in the mountains of Colorado and courses down through the heart of New Mexico until it leaves the state just beyond Las Cruces. From there it serves as a natural border between the United States and Mexico before dumping its water from the Southern Rockies into the Gulf of Mexico. The Rio Grande is the fourth largest river system in North America. Except where it is dammed at Cochiti Lake west of Santa Fe, the river is essentially free-flowing nearly all the way to Socorro, allowing it to fluctuate dramatically over the

THE BIG RIVER

The Rio Grande at flood stage,
June 6, 1993. WWD

seasons—from a raging torrent at the height of the snowmelt to a near trickle at the end of summer.

Lined by cottonwoods and willows along with introduced invasive Salt Cedars and Russian Olives, the Rio Grande mostly flows placidly through the shallow valley that is governed by the Rio Grande Rift. But northwest of Taos it has carved down through layers of volcanic basalt rock, reaching a breath-taking depth of eight hundred feet in its gorge. Just west of Taos a highway bridge—at six hundred and fifty feet, the third highest bridge in the United States—spans the river. The first sixty-eight miles of flowing water after it enters New Mexico has been designated a National Wild and Scenic River and is known for its world-class white-water rafting and kayaking.

Gallery forests found along the floodplains of streamsides and riverbanks in the Southwest are known as bosques—a Spanish word for woodlands. The one hundred and eighty miles of the Rio Grande from Cochiti Reservoir to well past Socorro is perhaps *the* classic bosque. Except for a few breaks, the river is lined on both sides by dense vegetation that hosts an array of riparian-loving birds and wildlife.

Fires, water diversion, and the spread of alien tree species have become a serious threat to the Rio Grande Bosque. Rio Grande Valley Cottonwoods are in particular jeopardy because natural regeneration is not replacing the forty- to eighty-year-old trees that now dominate the floodplain. An interagency Rio Grande Bosque Initiative was established in 1993 to address this and the many human-caused problems.

The Rio Grande State Park, north and south of and through Albuquer-que, manages and protects an urban wilderness. Probably the easiest place to experience the bosque is at the Rio Grande Nature Center in the heart of the city. Mesilla Bosque State Park outside of Las Cruces and Bosque del Apache National Wildlife Refuge south of Socorro are other locations where you can learn about these natural treasures.

Between Colorado and Texas only three major tributaries feed into the Rio Grande—the Red and Chama rivers up north and the Rio Puerco in the center of the state. The one-hundred-fifty-mile-long Rio Puerco (filthy river) is without a doubt the preeminent example of riparian degradation in New Mexico, if not the nation. This so-called river gained national notoriety for having carried the densest-known load of suspended sediments of any stream in the U.S. Overgrazing by sheep around the turn of the nineteenth century was the culprit. Those five million sheep in the 1890s were devastating to our grasslands. With the land stripped of cover to impede water runoff during storms, flash floods became commonplace, and the tremendous erosional

ELEPHANT BUTTE RESERVOIR

Named for a volcanic rock formation, now an island, that is supposed
to resemble an elephant, Elephant
Butte Reservoir was created in 1916
by a dam constructed across the Rio
Grande. Forty miles long with more
than two hundred miles of shoreline,
it's New Mexico's largest body of
water and the state's most popular
water recreation facility. When visita-
tion approaches one hundred thousand over the Memorial Day weekend,
the state park here hosts about the
same number of people as live in Las
Cruces, our second largest city. Truth
or Consequences, the gateway town
to the park, was named for Ralph
Edwards's radio quiz show, a relic of
the past that only a few modern visitors (including the author) will recall.

Elephant Butte Reservoir. Photo: Angele Majewicz

power of rapidly flowing water carved the continuous, deep, often straight
trench that the Rio Puerco trickles through today.

Flowing water is what enticed Pueblo Indians to move from places like
Chaco and Mesa Verde to our major river valleys centuries before the Spaniards arrived on the scene. They needed a reliable supply of water to nourish
their fields of corn, beans, squash, and, in the south, cotton, for these people
had long been accomplished farmers. All nineteen of New Mexico's living
pueblos are located on or very near water flowing through the Great Basin
Grassland ecoregion.

SALT MISSIONS TRAIL
NATIONAL SCENIC BYWAY

TRAVERSING THE HEART of New Mexico from the mountains to the plains, the Salt Missions Trail threads along the eastern foothills of the Manzano (apple) Mountains through Piñon-Juniper Woodlands and open grassy flats. You'll see Alligator Junipers, named for their bark that resembles an alligator's hide, as well as One-seed Junipers—the common juniper in the central part of the state. Here all junipers are usually called "cedars."

Take the gravel loop road that penetrates the lower slopes of these mountains to Fourth of July Canyon in mid-October and you'll get to enjoy one of our state's most vivid fall color displays—the fiery red hues of Bigtooth Maple on either side of the road.

Back along the main route, the village of Manzano is the location where the early Spaniards first planted an apple orchard in the 1620s. Apples are an Old World fruit that arrived in New Mexico with the first Spanish colonists. In fact, most of the fruits we enjoy today, including bananas, peaches, cherries, apricots, and all the citrus fruits, originally were absent in the Americas; all were introduced by Columbus and his followers.

This scenic byway leads to the spectacular ruins of several missions that were constructed by Spanish Franciscan missionaries in the 1600s and which are now included in a unit of our National Park System. One of the old missions, Gran Quivira, is the largest ruin of any Christian church in the U.S., and another, Abo, is one of the most beautiful.

(opposite)
Alligator Juniper, named for its bark that resembles alligator hide. CCB

Bigtooth Maple lines a trail in Fourth of July Canyon. Photo: Gail DellaPelle

The ruins of Quari Mission, constructed in 1632, can be seen along the Salt Missions Trail Scenic Byway. WWD

4 GREAT PLAINS GRASSLAND

FIRST
IMPRESSIONS

The Great Plains Grassland ecoregion features pure stands of Blue Grama and other warm-season grasses. WWD

THE GRASSLANDS THAT OCCUPY most of the eastern half of our state typically consist of nearly pure stands of grass with few shrubs and virtually no trees except in the bottomlands. This land tends to be flat or rolling terrain, less defined by mountains or rock outcrops than our other major ecoregions.

The farther east you go, the thicker the grass, it seems. Shrubs such as mesquite and yucca become more obvious as you travel south. True prairie conditions more often occur east of the Pecos and Canadian rivers, and some ecologists consider those rivers to form the natural western boundary of the Great Plains Grassland. For the purpose of this book, however, I have elected to include in this ecoregion everything east of the Sangre de Cristo, Sandia, Manzano, and Sacramento mountain ranges south to where the Chihuahuan Desert takes over. All of this landscape has a similar feel to it.

This is rangeland rather than farmland, so you'll never have to drive far to encounter a herd of cattle. Except for a few small towns such as Clayton, Tucumcari, Clovis, and Hobbs, the eastern third of this grassland is sparsely populated, though ranch homes dot the countryside everywhere and barbed-wire fences delineating range units crisscross the land.

If ever there were a land of "Big Sky," this is it.

(previous)
Bottomless Lakes. CCB

Hereford cattle grazing the shortgrass prairie. WWD

SHORTGRASS PRAIRIE

PRECIPITATION INCREASES EASTWARD across the Great Plains, reaching nearly thirty inches a year on its eastern margin, where the original famous tallgrass prairie has largely been converted into our corn belt, the breadbasket of America. In New Mexico we are dealing with the western subdivision of the Great Plains—the shortgrass prairie that stretches from Canada to our southern border and occupies much of Montana, eastern Wyoming, eastern Colorado, eastern New Mexico, and the panhandles of Oklahoma and Texas. Native grasses are, indeed, much shorter here than in the mixed-grass and tallgrass prairies farther east.

Two plants dominate the plant cover here—Blue Grama and Buffalo Grass. Blue Grama, our official state grass, is probably the commonest native grass in New Mexico, growing in virtually every county. An ankle-high or somewhat taller bunchgrass with eyebrow-shaped seed heads, Blue Grama spreads in clumps. It's the food of choice for range cattle today just as it was for the bison that roamed across the shortgrass prairie in the distant past.

Buffalo Grass, barely six inches tall, is a true sod-forming species. It puts out horizontal stems that can grow an inch or two a day as the runners creep along the ground, worming their way through the soil. Buffalo Grass forms dense mats that exclude all other plants. Its roots extend up to six feet underground and then branch out, growing horizontally for several feet. The roots may comprise ninety percent of each plant's total bulk. Grazing has always played an important role in maintaining both of these grasses.

Most species in the shortgrass prairie are warm-season grasses that green up in early summer and don't reach full maturity until late July or

August, right after the monsoon rains have soaked the ground. With the panoply of green grass, golden roadside sunflowers, and blue skies, late summer is the best time of year to become immersed in the open vistas of our shortgrass prairie.

Shrubs tend to be scarce on these grasslands, but driving east from Roswell on U.S. 380, you'll suddenly come upon a forest of low-growing shrub-like oaks where grasses are almost nonexistent. If you thought that all oaks are trees, think again, for the Shinnery Oak in the "forest" here isn't quite as tall as a person, though the root system of a single tree can extend more than fifty feet through the dune sand to reach moisture. Pure stands of Shinnery Oak extend over a vast expanse of rolling dunes known as the Mescalero Sands. These oak-covered sands are home to the Lesser Prairie Chicken, a bird that was so ubiquitous during the nineteenth century that millions of them were shipped back east to serve as delicacies in fancy restaurants. Today this bird has become an endangered species throughout its range.

In the early days dryland farming was unsuccessful on this part of the prairie because rainfall during the growing season was much too iffy. But in parts of Colorado, Kansas, Oklahoma, and Texas the shortgrass prairie had been plowed at one time, allowing the drought and ferocious winds of the 1930s dust bowl years to erode most of the bare topsoil and send it to the heavens.

Blue Grama is the most common native grass in New Mexico. WWD

Shinnery Oak "forest" east of Roswell. CCB

KIOWA NATIONAL GRASSLANDS

Located in the far northeast corner of our state just east of Clayton, the eastern section of the Kiowa National Grasslands preserves some of the best examples of shortgrass prairie anywhere. Administered by the U.S. Forest Service, these national grasslands consist of numerous small parcels that are being moderately grazed today. The area was devastated during the dust bowl years, but it has recovered under government supervision to the point where carpets of native grass and wildflowers prevail, and wildlife is abundant. In addition to the natural environment, it's the best place I know of to see and photograph all kinds of windmills—some still operating, others relics from the past.

Relic windmill at Clayton. Photo: Vangie Dunmire

PRAIRIE ANIMALS OTHER THAN DOMESTIC LIVESTOCK, pronghorn (popularly known as antelope, though they are more closely related to deer than to the true antelopes of Africa) are the largest mammals inhabiting most of the shortgrass prairie. Two white throat patches and a large white rump patch on a tan animal are a dead giveaway. Built for speed, pronghorn are the fastest animals in the Western Hemisphere and have been clocked at up to seventy miles per hour for minutes at a time. They graze on the grass in herds of twenty or more.

A remarkable diversity of wildlife inhabits this prairie, and some of the animals are ecologically connected. Blacktail Prairie Dogs thrive on these grasslands and live in "towns" that often contain hundreds of residents. These large ground squirrels are most often seen sitting straight up on bare mounds of earth surrounding their burrows. Burrowing Owls, which are less than a foot tall, frequently occupy abandoned prairie dog burrows. The adults perch on the mounds, then fly out to capture insects and small rodents, bringing them to the baby owls being raised down in the burrows. Rattlesnakes also use prairie dog burrows for winter denning. Though most people fear these snakes, human bites are rare and almost never fatal. You practically have to step on one to get bitten.

Expect to see Meadow Larks, Horned Larks, and other ground-hugging birds in abundance. But some other bird species will surprise you. Potholes and swales attract all kinds of shorebirds and even ducks, geese, and, occasionally, cranes. This is hawk paradise with more than a dozen species that soar over the prairie at different times of the year.

For thousands of years as many as thirty million American Bison held sway across the grasslands of the Great Plains. Bison were probably the most numerous single species of large mammal on earth at the time. In New Mexico they grazed upon the shortgrass prairie but never did reach the Rio Grande or points west. By the late 1800s they were gone, having fallen prey to heavy commercial-market hunting and the wanton killing of bison, a national policy intended to starve the Plains Indians into submission. As bison numbers waned, domestic cattle took their place as the principal herbivore on the eastern grasslands, becoming a seemingly natural element of our living landscape.

Pronghorn on the shortgrass prairie. WWD

A Burrowing Owl spooks a prairie dog. Photo: Pat Gaines

Arrival of the Anglo Cattleman

As was true throughout the New Mexico Territory, sheep had been herded by Hispanic families on the eastern plains for many decades, though not nearly in the numbers that grazed in the Rio Grande Valley or in the higher country west of the river. Following the Civil War when two ranchers from Texas, Charles Goodnight and Oliver Loving, discovered that driving cattle into New Mexico and selling them for a handsome profit was a good deal, life on our prairies was never quite the same again. Their trackway, used year after year, became known as the Goodnight-Loving Trail, and in 1874 more than one hundred thousand cattle were driven through Roswell on their way up the Pecos River. It was the largest number that had traversed New Mexico in a single season up to that time.

By the end of the century the cattle population in the Territory of New Mexico had risen to well over a million head, and the open range had given way to cattle ranches completely fenced with barbed wire, just as we see it today. I've come to learn that cattle ranchers here are some of the friendliest folks in the state. If you step out of your vehicle to examine these grasslands up close, a nearby rancher is likely to drive over and ask you if you need help. Once he sees that you're not up to any mischief, he'll probably tell you all about the countryside and perhaps a little about ranching on the prairie these days.

MORE VOLCANOES AND OTHER GEOLOGIC FORMATIONS

MOST OF THE SHORTGRASS PRAIRIE is relatively flat, but New Mexico's volcanic past has produced some interesting land features. Up north, U.S. 64/87 from Raton to Clayton threads between two of them. North of this highway, Capulin Mountain is the cone of a volcano that was active about ten thousand years ago. A road to the summit takes you to a trailhead where you can walk right into the cone. Capulin Mountain, protected as one of New Mexico's several national monuments, is one of the few places in the world where such a thing can be done.

South of the highway, Sierra Grande, a gently sloping dome that rises 2,200 feet above the surrounding plain is the largest volcano in the northern part of our state. This mountain is a shield volcano that formed from countless eruptions of molten basalt lava which then spread across the landscape in flat sheets. Mauna Loa on the Big Island in Hawaii, the world's largest active volcano, probably is the best-known example of a shield volcano. At an elevation of 8,720 feet, the summit of Sierra Grande is the easternmost point in the U.S. that rises more than 8,000 feet above sea level.

Forty-three miles north of Las Vegas, on I-25, Wagon Mound is named for its shape, which resembles an old Con-

Cattle country along I-25 north of Las Vegas. CCB

estoga wagon. It was once an important landmark for covered wagons and traders that plied the Santa Fe Trail. The butte itself, towering over the village of the same name, is the cap of an ancient lava flow and has been designated a National Historic Landmark.

Far to the south, an astonishing array of geological features is preserved at Bottomless Lakes State Park, a few miles east of Roswell. The lakes here are actually deep sinkholes that were formed when circulating underground water dissolved salt and gypsum deposits to form subterranean caverns. When the cavern roofs collapsed from their own weight, sinkholes resulted and soon filled with water. The greenish-blue hues of the water are caused by algae and other aquatic plants covering the lake bottoms. Two of the lakes are ninety feet deep, and each of them displays its own particular beauty. This area is famous for "Pecos Diamonds"—quartz crystals formed inside the gypsum deposits.

Along our eastern border the Llano Estacado (staked plains, though how it got its name is unclear) is a level, treeless, elevated plain surrounded by escarpments fifty to three hundred feet high on three sides. U.S. 70/84 approaching Clovis ascends to it as does U.S. 380 east from Roswell after leaving the dense stands of Shinnery Oak along the way. The entire Llano covers more area than all of New England combined, but most of the tableland is in Texas, where cotton farming prevails. In 1541, Francisco Coronado wrote, "I reached some plains so vast, that I did not find their limit anywhere I went, although I travelled over them for more than 300 leagues . . . with no more land marks than if we had been swallowed up by the sea. . ."

In New Mexico the Llano has been described as "eighty-five percent sky and fifteen percent grass."

Sierra Grande—a shield volcano. CCB

The Wagon Mound formation was an important landmark along the Santa Fe Trail. CCB

RIVERS COURSING THE GRASSLAND

MOST OF THE SO-CALLED RIVERS in this ecoregion that are shown on the Official Highway Map of New Mexico hardly ever flow except after monsoon downpours, and nearly all the lakes are actually man-made dammed reservoirs. However, two major rivers—the Pecos and the Canadian—do carry a substantial flow of water down from the Sangre de Cristo Mountains west of the plains.

The Pecos River originates above the town of Pecos, then spills out onto the shortgrass prairie, where it winds through the flatlands in a barely discernable broad valley. The river continues flowing south to where it leaves the state at 2,841 feet elevation, the lowest point in the state. It finally feeds into the Rio Grande in Texas, more than 900 miles from its source.

In 1541, Coronado may have been the first Spaniard to cross this river. He and his retinue built a flimsy bridge across the river at a point south of present-day Santa Rosa and later made an encampment at Pecos Pueblo near the present town. More than three centuries later, the first Texas longhorn cattle were driven up the river along the Goodnight-Loving Trail.

Bottomless Lakes, established in 1933, was New Mexico's first state park. CCB

SANTA FE TRAIL
NATIONAL SCENIC BYWAY

FROM 1821, when the first train of pack animals left Missouri bound for Santa Fe, until 1880, a span of sixty years, the Santa Fe Trail moved men, trade goods, and, later, emigrants, across the continent. The trail automatically became linked to El Camino Real, the Spanish Royal Road which led to Chihuahua, Zacatecas, and Mexico City far to the south, providing new markets for merchants in New Mexico as well as Mexico. It remained active until the completion of the first railroad to Santa Fe made it instantly obsolete in 1880.

The main trail entered New Mexico over Raton Pass, while the shorter but more hazardous Cimarron Cutoff entered the state north of present-day Clayton. The Santa Fe Trail National Scenic Byway travels west out of Clayton, passing Rabbit Ear Mountain, an important landmark on the trail. Wagon Mound was the last major landmark before the trail's destination point in Santa Fe. The wagon wheels cut deep ruts in the prairie sod—ruts that eventually broadened into a trough that could be hundreds of feet wide. Scars from the trail can still be seen in places along the route, one of the best being on the Kiowa National Grasslands north of Clayton.

Evidence of the famous trail is also visible at Fort Union, where both branches of it merged from the east. Fort Union dates back to the 1850s and is now a national monument just off I-25 a few miles north of Las Vegas. The old fort was headquarters for U.S. Army troops, who carried out relentless campaigns against marauding Apache, Comanche, and other prairie Indians. It later became a sprawling installation serving as the principal supply base for the Military Department of New Mexico.

Fort Union Ruins. Photo: Erin Willett

5 PIÑON-JUNIPER WOODLANDS

FIRST
IMPRESSIONS

S O OFTEN WHEN DRIVING across New Mexico's grassy plains the highway
will rise a bit and suddenly you see juniper shrubs or trees dotting the
landscape. If the road continues to climb a hill or mesa or is heading toward a
range of mountains, the trees will thicken, and low-growing Piñon Pines will
be added to the mix. Now you've entered a different ecoregion—the Piñon-
Juniper Woodlands. Most of us just call it P/J for short.

You'll notice that almost no other kinds of trees grow here, though the
ground can be densely covered with shrubs and grass. The soil is thin, rocky,
and often exposed, leading to obvious erosion where the terrain is steep.

(opposite)
Photo: David Cramer

(previous)
Thunderstorm over
San Ysidro. WWD

PIÑON-JUNIPER WOODLANDS ECOREGION

THIS IS A TRANSITION ZONE between the higher elevation forests and drier grassy plains below. It has an overstory of Piñon Pines combined with one or more species of juniper—often widely scattered. Such open woodlands occur in most every part of the state except for the far eastern shortgrass prairie, and even there an occasional juniper may pop up. About a quarter of the land in our state is classified as Piñon-Juniper Woodlands.

Whether driving along New Mexico's interstates or on any number of lesser state or federal highways, the most conspicuous trees within or at the edge of our grasslands and deserts are stragglylooking junipers. Along with pines, firs, and spruce, junipers are conifers, but instead of needles they have overlapping scales for leaves and tiny seedbearing cones that resemble small berries. Utah Junipers with their pea-size cone berries prevail in the Four Corners region, Alligator Junipers with distinctive checkered bark grow in the south, and One-seed Junipers are found nearly everywhere. Don't look for juniper berries on all the trees because junipers are dioecious, with about half of them being female and producing berries and the other half pollen-bearing males. Male trees are easily identified in spring when heavy orange pollen transforms them—and is the bane of those who suffer allergies.

Birds are the most important dispersers of juniper seeds, and seeds that have passed through the digestive tract of a bird such as a robin germinate faster than uneaten seeds. Piñon Jays and Scrub Jays are the principal planters of the seeds.

Piñon-Juniper Woodlands. WWD

One-seed Juniper berries. WWD

Junipers can grow under more arid conditions than Piñon Pines, thus piñons may not be part of the mix at the lower edge of these woodlands. In fact, vast expanses of juniper-dotted grasslands, called juniper savannas, occur throughout the state. But as the road traveled gains elevation, piñons enter the picture to the point where they can make up a pure, dense forest at the upper end of the P/J zone.

Prehistoric Indians were custodians of a once vast piñon and juniper "orchard" that provided them with food, fuel, building material, tools, and medicine. These woodlands, where most of the Puebloan villages were (and still are) located in our state, have provided basic nourishment for the people from before the time they were first experimenting with the cultivation of corn right up to the present.

Piñon Pine, the state tree of New Mexico, is easy to distinguish from other pines, since the needles are short and clustered in twos. Their lower stature and rounded crowns almost always give them away. Small, compact cones require three growing seasons to mature and produce pea-size nuts. In any given location a bumper crop of piñon nuts can be expected only about every six years.

With more than three thousand calories per pound, piñon nuts have been the most valuable local wild-plant food source for Indians living in New Mexico during prehistoric and recent historic times. For them, the piñon was the tree of life. Indeed, the biological value of its protein on a per-pound basis is comparable to beefsteak and exceeds that of all commercial nuts with the exception of the cashew. Each nut also contains all twenty amino acids that make up protein, and of the nine amino acids essential to human growth, seven are more concentrated in piñon nuts than in corn.

Miscellaneous uses of piñon by Indians are legion and include making blue-green pottery paint from boiling the gum as well as producing an all-purpose glue by warming the pitch. Piñon craft continues in the Navajo tradition, with the pitch used to make a black dye and for giving Navajo wickerwork its shine. Parts of the piñon are used for medicine in nearly every Navajo healing ceremony.

Piñons are slow-growing and long-lived. Trees that are three hundred to four hundred years old are common, and some have survived longer than five hundred years—even up to one thousand. More often a bark beetle infestation will kill off the older trees, leaving skeleton trees among the junipers. The worst die-off in recent years occurred between 2002 and 2003 when forty to eighty percent of the piñons were done in throughout the Southwest. Those were drought years, and high temperatures coupled with lack of moisture made the trees vulnerable to insects. Bark beetles delivered the knockout punch. The effect was so dramatic that it could be detected by satellites.

Less than a thousand years ago when ancestral Puebloans began to build their cities of adobe and their population expanded, ever more wood needed to be cut for cooking and heating fuel as well as for new construction. That seems to have resulted in a reduction of many of these woodlands—at least the mature tree component. Both piñons and junipers are fire-sensitive, and wildfires also played a role.

But during the past century, when Puebloans and others had less need for fuelwood and wildfire suppression became a national priority, junipers

Piñon Pine loaded with developing cones. WWD

have been invading New Mexico's grasslands to the point where livestock grazing has been affected. Nowadays land managers are employing a number of strategies to reverse this trend.

UNDERSTORY PLANTS OF THE WOODLANDS

OTHER THAN TREES, which are scarce on the grassy plains that surround our P/J lands, most of the same plants typical of the grasslands occur in the woodlands as well but at slightly higher elevations. Both cool-season grasses such as Indian Ricegrass and New Mexico Feathergrass (see page 59) and warm-season grasses—for example, several species of grama and bluestem—grow among the piñon and junipers. When it matures at the end of summer, Side-oats Grama adds a bronze tint to the landscape.

A great variety of shrubs and grasses comprise the understory of our P/J Woodlands. During a plant survey on a square mile of public open space near Albuquerque, I once identified twenty-three species of native shrubs and forty-three different grasses, only nine of which were introduced from elsewhere.

Where soils are sandy, Sand Sagebrush often graces the hillsides. It's related to Big Sagebrush, so dominant in the Great Basin Desert, but with a willowy form and threadlike smoky blue leaves, it's a much more attractive shrub.

It's not always easy to hike cross-country in the P/J zone, for this is the shrubbiest of all our ecoregions. Dense thickets of Gambel Oak or Mountain Mahogany are commonplace, often the result of rapid establishment following long-ago forest fires.

Many of the woodland shrubs display colorful blossoms. In spring Feather Indigobush, a two-foot-tall shrub with tiny pink-and-yellow petals, grows in colonies on rocky hillsides. Chamisa, along with Three-leaf Sumac, with their respective golden and lovely reddish foliage, never fail to brighten up the countryside from late summer into fall.

Side-oats Grama, a warm-season grass. WWD

WILDFLOWERS APLENTY

OF ALL NEW MEXICO'S ECOREGIONS, the P/J Woodlands often present the best and longest-lasting display of wildflowers that are able to survive on barely sufficient moisture. This was borne out during a two-mile plant walk near my home in Placitas (just north of Albuquerque) that I led in May 2010, when we photographed more than thirty species of multicolored wildflowers in bloom. Among the commonest were Plains Blackfoot, Scorpionweed, White Milkwort, Bluets, Desert Marigold, Woolly Locoweed, and Indian Paintbrush. While hiking across the rocky slopes we were never far from both Piñon Pines and

Indian Paintbrush. WWD

Scorpionweed prefers sandy soils in the Piñon-Juniper Woodlands ecoregion. WWD

Cane Cholla. WWD

Claret-cup Cactus. WWD

One-seed Junipers. In other years this same plant walk has delivered far fewer plants in flower. So much depends upon recent moisture.

July and August monsoon rains prolong the show in most years, with different species of plants blooming through the summer and into fall. More and more of them tend to be yellow-flowered in the Sunflower family as the season wears on.

It might surprise you to learn that this is cactus-rich country, second only to the Chihuahuan Desert in our state. Cane Cholla, the tall, cylindrical species with magenta blossoms that often invades our grasslands, thrives on rocky P/J soils, but plants may die out if they become too shaded from encroaching tall shrubs or trees, making them a sentinel of land disturbance by human habitation or overgrazing. The commonest cacti here are several species of low-growing Prickly Pear Cactus that have yellowish flowers and stout-spined stems arranged in a series of pads. But the most spectacular of all in this zone is the Claret-cup Cactus with its several ribbed columnar stems. You won't miss these beauties if they're in bloom, for their brilliant red flowers are bound to catch anyone's eye.

PRICKLY PEAR CACTUS

More than one hundred species of prickly pear grow in the Western Hemisphere. Their large, fleshy fruits, called tunas, furnished food for any number of prehistoric Indians. In Mexico the ancient Aztecs recognized thirteen varieties of prickly pear tunas—some sour, some sweet; some eaten raw, others cooked. Prickly pear tunas were one of the few sweets available to natives living in New Mexico before the coming of the Spaniards, for neither sugarcane nor European honey bees had yet arrived on the continent.

Prickly Pear Cactus. WWD

PIÑON-JUNIPER ANIMAL LIFE

MOST OF THE LARGER MAMMALS here also range into the adjacent vegetation zones. Coyotes are equally at home in these woodlands and in nearby grasslands or deserts below the P/J. As winter approaches, Mule Deer drift down from the higher terrain. It would be most unusual, but a wonderful treat, to spot a Mountain Lion, even though our woodlands and lower forests are home to a surprising number of them. Catching a glimpse of a Bobcat is far more likely. At some point during your travels you are almost certain to see a Rock Squirrel skittering across the road. These bushy-tailed ground squirrels aren't shy, and they regularly burrow under outbuildings in rural areas.

Though nearly all livestock on our rangelands have owners, you might be lucky enough to catch a glimpse of our so-called "wild horses." Occasional bands of short-legged feral mustangs—typically a stallion with half a dozen mares—still roam on public lands and Indian reservations in parts of rural New Mexico. Recent blood tests of horses from one of these wild bands wan- est of Albuquerque showed that some of the animals to original Spanish stock.

Placitas, untamed mustangs, apparently long ago Felipe Pueblo Reservation, still move skittishly yside and are a regular topic of community chitchat. eat (the horse lovers) or a great nuisance (some of

"Wild" horses roam on the hills of Placitas. Photo: David Cramer

More than seventy species of birds breed in the P/J Woodlands, and a number of them rarely leave this zone. Some, like migrating Western Blue-birds, Mountain Bluebirds, and Cedar Waxwings rely on juniper berries for food. Juniper mistletoe, a common parasite on these trees, also bears tiny translucent berries that are an important food source for birds. Juncos are the most ubiquitous year-round birds in these woodlands, but they are also about as common in the Montane Forest above. However, the Juniper Titmouse and the Piñon Jay, neither of which migrate, are two species that strictly inhabit P/J country.

Every summer plants with nectar-producing blossoms attract a parade of hummingbirds to the woodlands. Broad-tailed and Black-chinned Hummingbirds arrive first and remain until fall. In late July or August, Rufous Hummingbirds turn up, and the aggressive males try to shoo off all the others from every flower (or feeder) it seems. Several other hummingbird species may be seen in the woodlands of our Chihuahuan Desert down south.

Red-tailed Hawks and Common Ravens soar overhead. In the past dozen years, White-winged Doves, a bird formerly limited to the Chihuahuan and Sonoran deserts, have invaded the grasslands and woodlands as far north as Santa Fe—another outcome of global warming, I believe.

NEW MEXICO'S WEATHER PATTERNS

JULY AND AUGUST, when monsoon moisture sweeps up from the gulfs of Mexico and California, are the rainiest months over most of the state. The advent of the monsoon in early July is the most predictable weather event in New Mexico. Thirty to forty percent of a year's total moisture typically falls during those two months. Summer thunderstorms tend to be brief but intense.

PIÑON JAY

This chunky bluish-gray jay is highly social and is normally seen in flocks of twenty or more birds, most of them squawking up a storm. Their behavior is specialized to exploit piñon nuts for food, but they also seek out fruits and berries along with insects and spiders. They have a mutual relationship with Piñon Pines: the trees provide these birds with food, nesting, and roosting sites, while the jays promote pine reproduction. That's because Piñon Jays have a habit of caching pine nuts on the ground for later use. One to seven nuts are placed in each cache, and a single jay can cache more than twenty thousand seeds in a season. Of course, not all the nuts are recovered, allowing a few to germinate into new pine seedlings.

Piñon Jay. Photo: Kurt Hasselman

In fact, the highest thunderstorm frequency in all the United States during July and August is along the Colorado–New Mexico border. With such an extreme incidence of these storms, no wonder we have the dubious distinction of having the greatest per capita death rate from lightning in the nation.

Winter precipitation results from the inland movement of Pacific storms, but not much of it reaches our lower elevations. Winter is the driest season in much of the state with the exception of the western slopes along the Continental Divide, where snow can accumulate to great depths.

Global climate cycles that affect the Pacific Ocean greatly influence seasonal weather here. An event known as El Niño, when tropical seawater temperatures rise, results in the Southwest having a wetter winter. Conversely, during La Niña years, when water temperatures become significantly lower, our winters are much drier—not a good thing for a state that continually worries about having sufficient water. La Niña was particularly harsh in 2011, resulting in severe drought throughout the state.

Scrub Jay. WWD
Photo: Bob Barber

TURQUOISE TRAIL
NATIONAL SCENIC BYWAY

NAMED FOR THE RICH TURQUOISE deposits that are concentrated in the hills along this route, the Turquoise Trail winds through colorful Piñon-Juniper Woodlands on its way to or from Santa Fe. Linking Albuquerque with Santa Fe, State Road 14 is a pleasurable option to driving the much more direct interstate. Rolling rocky terrain and cultural history deliver the color.

Mining is one focus of this journey. The ghost town of Golden was named in the 1880s for the imagined mother lode that was never discovered here. Coal was what brought miners to establish the village of Madrid, which began to boom soon after the first railroad reached Santa Fe in 1880. But it was turquoise that really put this region on the map.

Ancestral Puebloans began to mine that mineral in the Cerrillos Hills as early as AD 900, crafting it into jewelry and mosaics at Chaco, the center of civilization at the time. Blue gemstones collected here eventually made their way to Spain, where early on they were added to the crown jewel collection.

Among the several villages on this route, Madrid (locally pronounced with the accent on the first syllable) is the draw for tourists in summer. When artists and craftspeople arrived in the 1970s, the village was transformed into a delightful showcase of quirky storefronts, taverns, and the Old Coal Mine Museum, along with a lot of arts-and-crafts studios and shops.

Turquoise mining site in the Cerrillos Hills along the Turquoise Trail National Scenic Byway. CCB

(left)
Upper Falls, Frijoles Canyon, Bandelier National Monument. WWD

6 MONTANE FORESTS

FIRST
IMPRESSIONS

Truchas Peaks southwest of Taos. CCB

APART FROM OUR DESERTS AND GRASSY PLAINS, New Mexico is, after all, a land of mesas and mountains. None are as tall as the fifty-four peaks rising more than fourteen thousand feet above sea level in Colorado or the fourteen equally tall summits in California, but countless mountains here do rise above ten thousand feet.

But high elevation is not what distinguishes the Montane Forest ecoregion. It's the solid stands of evergreen conifers that define it. You'll know that you have entered this ecoregion when the road becomes hemmed in by much taller trees than the piñons and junipers below. A glance at the map (see page 12) will make clear how widespread this ecoregion is in the state.

Whereas our deserts and grasslands tend to have fairly uniform vegetation across wide expanses, changes in plant cover are often abrupt up higher. That becomes apparent as you gain or lose elevation when driving our mountain roads. In fact, for each thousand-foot rise in elevation, the average temperature drops more than three degrees Fahrenheit and annual precipitation from rain and snow increases about four inches—a combination that results in more available moisture for plants during the growing season.

(previous)
The Lone Ranger. CCB

Snow in the high country,
May 11, 2010. CCB

MONTANE FOREST ECOREGION

ABOVE THE PIÑON-JUNIPER WOODLANDS, the mountain ranges of New Mexico display a truly astonishing diversity of coniferous forests. Between Taos and Santa Fe the high country is a southern extension of the Rocky Mountain chain that forms the backbone of America, but you can also experience it traveling through similar evergreen forests on highways that traverse the Jemez, Sacramento, Sandia, and Mogollon mountains in other parts of the state.

Unlike New Mexico's five other ecoregions, the Montane Forest consists of a series of contrasting vegetation zones, each the product of increasing elevation and, thus, precipitation.

The Ponderosa Pine zone, roughly between 7,000 and 8,500 feet in central New Mexico, boasts the tallest trees—Ponderosa Pines, easily recognized by their reddish, puzzle-like bark smelling delightfully of vanilla and five-inch-long needles, three to a cluster. The trees are usually widely spaced, and openings between them tend to be grassy rather than shrubby, so it's usually fairly easy to walk cross-country in this zone. Due to past logging and forest fires, Ponderosa Pines in our state are seldom fully mature.

Ascending the mountains above 8,000 feet, pines give way to a much denser forest in what's known as the mixed conifer zone, where it is cooler and wetter throughout the year. Douglas-firs and White Firs, both having short, unclustered needles, dominate the landscape; shrubs and smaller trees of many different species fill in any open spaces on the ground. Where sunlight is abundant in openings created by past forest fires, winter avalanches, or other natural disasters, Gambel Oak or Quaking Aspen move in to fill the void. In fall, aspens contribute magnificent swatches of gold on many of our high mountain slopes.

During your travels you are likely to be driving for a longer time in the mixed conifer zone than in the zones above and below it, for this Douglas-fir forest is the most extensive cover type on our higher mountains.

The spruce-fir zone can occur above 9,000 feet, but more often it begins at around 10,000 feet and continues up to timberline. Engelmann Spruce and

Corkbark Firs take over, and a heavy accumulation of rotting needles, twigs, and wood restricts undergrowth. Timber blowdown, insect outbreaks, fire, and avalanches all affect the vegetation mosaic. Aspen groves and mountain meadows provide a delightful contrast to the often impenetrable thickets of timber. It's cold and windy here, and snow is likely to remain on the ground during most months of the year.

Not many of our highways ascend to this zone. Those that do include the roads on Sierra Blanca and through the village of Cloudcroft in the Sacramento Mountains down south; the Enchanted Circle Scenic Byway and some other roads east and west of Taos; the Jemez Mountain Trail National Scenic Byway; and the road to the Sandia Crest east of Albuquerque.

Our mountain streams and creeks provide conditions for contrasting vegetation. Permanently wet soil gives rise to thickets of willow, often with Mountain Alder or Chokecherry mixed in. Two trees in particular—Narrowleaf Cottonwood and Colorado Blue Spruce—have adapted to mountain streamsides in New Mexico. The smoky-blue foliage of the latter, a tall tree, is unmistakable. Because of its classic beauty, Colorado Blue Spruce has been designated the state tree of both Colorado and Utah.

Above timberline the alpine zone displays an ecosystem unlike any other. Trail Ridge Road, which climbs above 13,000 feet in Rocky Mountain National Park in Colorado, is the best place in America to experience the wonders of this environment by vehicle. Alas, none of New Mexico's paved roads penetrate the alpine zone, but many trails do, including several in the Pecos Wilderness and, of course, the one to the summit of Wheeler Peak, the highest point in the state.

The climb from Albuquerque to the crest of the Sandia Mountains serves as a good example of

Ponderosa Pines. CCB

*Mixed conifer forest in the
Jemez Mountains. WWD*

Mountain meadow on Cañada Bonito in the Jemez Mountains. WWD

these progressive zones. I-40 leaves the Great Basin Grassland and enters the Piñon-Juniper Woodland zone just beyond the city. The P/J belt that encircles the base of these mountains is fairly narrow here, and within a few miles after turning off the interstate on the road leading to the crest, taller Ponderosa Pines and feathery-leaved Rocky Mountain Junipers replace the piñons. Higher on the mountain the ponderosas drop out—replaced by a zone of mixed conifers that includes Douglas-firs and White Firs. Finally, approaching the crest, which at 10,678 feet is the summit of the Sandia Mountains, an entirely different forest made up of Limber Pine, Corkbark Fir, and Engelmann Spruce will be encountered. Characteristic shrubs and other plants similarly change with elevation.

Until the turn of the nineteenth century, frequent lightning-caused wildfires were an important natural component of our forest ecosystem. Low-intensity fires removed ground fuel, allowing Ponderosa Pines and other conifers to reach maturity, their crowns safely above the flames. Rare high-intensity fires opened up large tracts of forest where short-lived species such as aspen could take over. A perfect example is the beautiful Aspen Basin along the road to the Santa Fe Ski Area, where a hot fire removed thousands of acres of mixed conifer forest in 1891.

However, a century of concentrated forest-fire suppression caused the ecosystem to get out of whack and resulted in abnormally dense stands of trees. The unnatural fuel buildup allowed those fires that did get out of hand to become holocaustic conflagrations, and more forest than ever was lost.

Today our land management agencies are taking a more ecologically enlightened approach. Deliberately igniting fires to thin out the undergrowth

under carefully planned prescribed conditions, they are also allowing some lightning-ignited fires to burn, so long as such fires can be contained within boundaries and not threaten habitations or private land.

AS WOULD BE EXPECTED, AT HIGHER ELEVATIONS an entirely different set of wildflowers blooms in the Montane Forest. Most of the plants found here can't survive the arid conditions down below, whereas plants on the plains rarely reach the Montane Forest ecoregion. The mountain show usually doesn't begin until June, but it lasts until the first freeze in early fall.

    Driving through the heart of the forest, two red-flowered beauties—Scarlet Gilia and Scarlet Bugler, the latter a penstemon—are likely to catch your eye, and by getting out of your vehicle and taking a short walk anywhere in our forests, you are virtually certain to see a number of low plants or shrubs in bloom during the growing season.

Aspen are regenerating ten years after the Cerro Grande Fire that destroyed many homes in Los Alamos in 2000. WWD

MOUNTAIN WILDFLOWERS

Wild penstemons are plentiful in New Mexico and are a particular favorite of nature enthusiasts here. Penstemon is an unusually large genus of plants having more than two hundred and fifty species in East Asia and North America. Thirty-four of those species occur in our state, most of them in the mountains.

Wildflowers tend to be more widely spaced under the mountain forest canopy than in the P/J Woodlands or grasslands below. But in the open meadows look for yellow-orange flowered Mulesears or Arrowleaf Balsamroot growing in clusters along with a variety of other wildflowers that grow best in forest openings.

Scarlet Gilia. WWD

Arrowleaf Balsamroot graces our forest openings. WWD

NORTH AMERICA'S LARGEST NATIVE MAMMAL, the moose, doesn't occur as far south as New Mexico, but Rocky Mountain Elk are now thriving in our mountains. By 1909 native populations had become exterminated, then subsequent reintroduction programs gradually built up the herds to the point where close to seventy thousand elk now reside in the state. The Jemez Mountains, the San Juan Mountains near Chama, and meadows throughout the Carson National Forest are preferred habitats for elk today. Since elk seek out grass rather than other vegetation, look for herds grazing in mountain meadows rather than in the forest itself. In some places the herds have grown

ELK AND OTHER MOUNTAIN ANIMAL LIFE

Elk grazing in an open meadow below Eagle Nest Lake. CCB

Bull Elk. WWD

beyond the limits of their habitat due to the absence of their natural predator, the Gray Wolf.

Mule Deer are more widespread than elk and can be spotted almost anywhere in the lower reaches of our hills and mountains. Black Bears are seldom seen, though they, too, are commonplace. Most every summer a few loners will cause havoc in cities like Albuquerque or Santa Fe when they wander down from the mountains in search of garbage. Grizzly Bears no longer occur in the state, however.

Jays and related birds are the noisiest creatures in our high country, and three species make their home here. In ascending elevation order, look for blue-colored Scrub Jays, Piñon Jays, and Steller's Jays that seek out a variety of seeds, nuts, berries, and insects. Up higher in the spruce-fir zone, gray-bodied Clark's Nutcrackers—birds with white patches on black wings and tails—are the showiest bird of this jay group. Many different species of woodpeckers along with juncos, chickadees, and nuthatches also thrive in our forests.

SACRAMENTO MOUNTAINS CHECKERSPOT

High in the Sacramento Mountains near the town of Cloudcroft two thousand acres of alpine meadow are the only known habitat for the Sacramento Mountains Checkerspot butterfly. The entire range of this but-terfly covers only thirty-three square miles. Needing sunlight and open spaces, the butterflies are unable to travel through thickly wooded areas to reach new habitat. Although the populations are now threatened by community developments encroach-ing on their meadows and by grazing livestock, conservation plans have been developed to ensure the survival of this beautiful endangered species.

Sacramento Mountains Checkerspot Butterfly. Photo: Steve Cary

TURKEYS

Nowadays wild turkeys are found in virtually every state, and they've always been native to New Mexico. Sometime before AD 800, ancestral Puebloans began to live-capture wild turkeys, and before long generation after generation of fowl were being raised in rock pens, no doubt fed on surplus corn. Even in the wild, flocks of turkeys are unusu-ally tolerant of humans today, so if you spot one remain quiet and expect to see more of them—perhaps even a gobbler boldly displaying his fan of tail feathers. Nearly all our ranges support popula-tions of America's Thanksgiving symbol.

Wild turkey habitat. WWD

WATERWAYS AND WATERFALLS

SNOW MELTING ON OUR TALLEST MOUNTAINS and those in Colorado is the principal source of New Mexico's precious water supply. Streams cascade down almost every mountain canyon or gully from late winter until the snowpack finally melts in summer. Yet the combination of rivers, lakes, and reservoirs makes up only .002 percent of the state's total land surface—the lowest water-to-land ratio of all fifty states.

Water flowing from the mountains seeps down through a labyrinth of rock layers and eventually reaches one of the state's aquifers. But recent studies are showing that water in our aquifers is dwindling because these underground reservoirs are being pumped for human use faster than they are being recharged. The future of water supplies in this arid state is rapidly becoming New Mexico's most urgent management concern.

New Mexico is hardly known for its waterfalls, but the state is home to plenty of them, with several located in the vicinity of Taos and along the Enchanted Circle Scenic Byway. Brazos Falls south of Chama, dropping 1,800 feet in two tiers, is the tallest, but it only can be reached by trail, and that's true of most of the falls in the state. Doug Scott, New Mexico's waterfall guru, has mapped and photographed more than two hundred of them.

Nambé Falls, 100 feet high, is on Nambé Pueblo Indian land north of Santa Fe. Photo: Doug Scott

New Mexico's precious water supply, Carson National Forest. CCB

ENCHANTED CIRCLE
NATIONAL
SCENIC BYWAY

THIS EIGHTY-FOUR-MILE LOOP out of Taos, one of five scenic byways in the Montane Forests ecoregion, is northern New Mexico's most popular day trip. The route completely encircles Wheeler Peak, which at 13,161 feet is the state's highest summit. Many miles of road traverse our two highest forest vegetation zones, so even in summer daytime temperatures will be on the cool side. Volcanic rock formations abound, especially around the village of Red River, where miners extracted gold, silver, copper, and lead in the late 1800s. From Bobcat Pass (elevation 9,820 feet) vistas of surrounding snowy high peaks can take your breath away. This loop passes through a number of mountain villages, nearly all of which have a colorful historic past.

By all means take a short side trip to view the spectacular Rio Grande Gorge west of Taos. From the vehicle and pedestrian bridge you can peer straight down to the river flowing through a 650-foot-deep box canyon carved in basalt lava rock. You'll be surprised to pass a community comprised of "earth-ships" and other strange-looking homes meant to foster a self-sustaining lifestyle.

The palisades along the Enchanted Circle Scenic Byway. CCB

The Taos Box, a world-class stretch of whitewater west of Taos. CCB

HIGH ROAD TO TAOS **SCENIC BYWAY**

HIGH ROAD IS RIGHT, for the scenery along this winding mountain road includes more vistas of our highest summits than any other road in the state. From the Rio Grande Valley north of Santa Fe, the route travels up through rolling badland hills to where the Sangre de Cristo Mountains dominate the eastern skyline. The Jemez Mountains beyond the Rio Grande command the far western horizon.

Before arriving at the village of Truchas (trout), a colorful classic Hispanic cemetery on the roadside is well worth examining. Take the paved road into Truchas for a few blocks to get the feel of a Spanish Land Grant village established in the mid-1700s. A bit farther along the road, Las Trampas (the traps) boasts one of the finest surviving eighteenth-century churches in our state. North of this village, look for a wooden structure on the right side of the highway that is commonly found in northern New Mexico. Acting as an aqueduct, it's a Spanish-style canoa that conducts water along the acequia (community ditch) system.

Along much of this sixty-mile route to Taos the highway traverses a mixed conifer forest peppered with Quaking Aspens having gleaming white bark and fluttering leaves that are light green in summer and vivid gold in the fall. The High Road offers an unforgettable blend of natural and human history.

Sangre de Cristo Mountains. CCB

Working *canoa* aqueduct along the High Road. WWD

Rio Grande Valley vista from the High Road to Taos Scenic Byway. CCB

SANTA FE NATIONAL FOREST **SCENIC BYWAY**

IF YOU ARE VACATIONING in Santa Fe, consider driving up to the Santa Fe Ski Area via this fifteen-mile scenic byway. The road winds up a deep, forested canyon, then steeply horseshoes up more than 3,000 vertical feet to the base of the ski area at 10,350 feet. Quaking Aspens color the peaks in early October, and roadside turnouts provide ample opportunities to take in sweeping views at any time of year. The ski lifts rise another 1,700 feet, and one of them runs when fall colors are at their best as well as during the ski season.

Quaking Aspens, Santa Fe National Forest. Photo: Mary Wachs

SUNSPOT **NATIONAL SCENIC BYWAY**

Vista of the Tularosa Basin and White Sands from Sunspot. Photo: Pat Davies

THIS FOURTEEN-MILE ROAD from Cloudcroft to Sunspot may be short, but on a per-mile basis it's rich with spectacular views. The road follows the rim of the Sacramento Mountains through a mixed conifer forest of Douglas-fir, White Fir, Limber Pine, and Quaking Aspen, and turnouts along the byway provide splendid vistas of the Tularosa Basin and the world's largest gypsum dune field at White Sands National Monument far below.

The pavement ends at the Sunspot National Solar Observatory, where the telescopes, one of them buried two hundred feet beneath the surface of Sacramento Peak, point to the sun and study its corona and solar flares.

TRAIL OF THE MOUNTAIN SPIRITS **NATIONAL SCENIC BYWAY**

LIKE THE HIGH ROAD TO TAOS and the Enchanted Circle, most of the Trail of the Mountain Spirits Scenic Byway winds through mountains forested with a mix of evergreens. This ninety-three-mile scenic byway in southwestern New Mexico traverses the nation's first designated wilderness area, the Gila, and crosses the Continental Divide twice. The Gila is a bird-lovers' paradise; more than three hundred species, including a surprising number of hummingbirds, have been identified along the route.

With Gila Cliff Dwellings National Monument at one end of the byway and the Mimbres Valley at the other, prehistoric culture is a definite highlight. The prehistoric Pueblo Indians who tilled the land and built their stone houses in open caves were artisans who wove cotton blankets and made pottery. Some of the most distinguished pottery was crafted a thousand years ago by the Mimbres branch of this culture.

Silver City, the jumping-off point for this byway, is a mountain gem. Originally established as a mining town, enormous vacated copper mine pits still exist on the outskirts of the city. It has become a retirement mecca and a place where artists and artistic expression thrive.

Gila Cliff Dwellings National Monument.
Photo: Glenn Petrucci

7 **NEW MEXICO'S SCENIC BYWAYS**

THE NATIONAL SCENIC BYWAYS PROGRAM administered by the Federal Highway Administration was established to help recognize, preserve, and enhance selected roads throughout the country. To qualify as a National Scenic Byway, each route must exhibit superior natural, cultural, archaeological, or recreational features, or otherwise have outstanding scenic qualities. In view of the fact that only one hundred and fifty of them have been established throughout the country, New Mexico can be justly proud that seven of our byways have been accorded national status. Altogether twenty-five scenic byways have been designated in our state.

For this book I have elected to include twelve of those scenic byways that I believe best exemplify our living landscapes and that can be followed on easily traveled highways. Ten of these byways are closely associated with the state's six major ecoregions, and descriptions of them have been included in those particular chapters.

Two of our byways have been saved for this chapter, for they traverse more than one major ecoregion and seem to stand on their own.

(previous)
White Mesa. CCB

BILLY THE KID NATIONAL SCENIC BYWAY

NAMED FOR NEW MEXICO'S MOST NOTORIOUS OUTLAW, this eighty-four-mile loop combines human history with natural beauty.

The town of Lincoln, much of it now a part of Lincoln State Monument, was the stage for one of the last great gunfights in the Old West, and it was the

focal point for perhaps our single most violent episode, the Lincoln County War. The conflicting stories of Billy the Kid play out in Lincoln's preserved landmarks, a number of which are open to the public.

Along this route you travel through Great Plains Grasslands all the way up to higher vegetational zones of the Montane Forest. At 12,003 feet, snowcapped Sierra Blanca punctuates the western skyline. You can follow a winding road partway up the mountain to Ski Apache, the nation's southernmost ski area, now owned and operated by the Mescalero Apache tribe. The road to the ski area ascends through an elegant spruce-fir forest of both Engelmann and Blue Spruce as well as Corkbark Fir. But it's the view to the east—all the way to the distant prairie—that will truly take your breath away.

Ruidoso, with its Ruidoso Downs Racetrack and Hubbard Museum of the American West, is in the heart of horse country, and horse-breeding ranches are just one delightful element of the surrounding countryside's pastoral scene. Lush apple orchards along the Rio Bonito and Rio Hondo waterways burst into bloom in spring, then paint the landscape with gold and yellow hues in fall. Occasional small flocks of fenced-in sheep add to the bucolic atmosphere.

JEMEZ MOUNTAIN TRAIL NATIONAL SCENIC BYWAY

I'M SAVING THIS GEM UNTIL LAST, for of all the loop trips and scenic byways in New Mexico, this one is my absolute favorite. It offers a splendid combination of spectacular geology, human history, archaeology, and terrific scenery, and it fully deserves its national status. Whether you approach the trail from Santa Fe or Albuquerque, plan on making a day of it. Here I cover it as a clockwise loop starting in Bernalillo, fifteen miles north of Albuquerque. Not all of what I describe precisely follows the official byway.

First off, you will pass Zia Pueblo perched on a small mesa not far off the highway. It's just a short drive to get a closer look at one of New Mexico's most traditional and conservative pueblos. No casinos here!

Then the road heads straight for a large mesa that is covered by thick beds of pure white gypsum. The gypsum here is being mined for use in manufacturing wallboard, plaster, and other building materials, and over the years the mesa top has gradually been whittled down.

Historic town of Lincoln. CCB

Sierra Blanca punctuates the western skyline along the Billy the Kid National Scenic Byway. CCB

The Billy the Kid National Scenic Byway is horse country. CCB

Beyond the pastoral village of San Ysidro, named for the patron saint of farmers, State Route 4 follows along the Jemez River, past the pueblo of that name with its Walatoma Visitor Center featuring excellent displays that help visitors understand the Pueblo Indian view of ancient and modern life. Walatoma is one of the most effective visitor centers in the state. Small corn-fields along the way bear living proof of the single most important crop for all Pueblo Indians, from prehistoric times to the present. The brightly colored high cliffs west of the road are a composite of ancient sandstones that are topped by lava flows and ash deposits from the eruptions of Jemez Volcano a million years ago.

At the upper end of the river valley, Jemez State Monument features the remarkably beautiful ruins of a mission that was built four hundred years ago by Spanish Franciscans next to the Indian pueblo that was located here at the time.

Shortly after ascending into a narrower canyon, travelers like to stop at the Soda Dam, where the precipitation of minerals from a collection of hot springs has formed a barrier to the river. Tiny ears of corn discovered in a

White Mesa with its cliffs of pure gypsum. CCB

nearby cave confirm that this region has been occupied for more than two thousand years.

The road then climbs steadily from P/J Woodlands through an impressive stand of Ponderosa Pines to a forest of mixed conifers and open meadows, and finally to the rim of Valles Caldera in the heart of Valles Grandes National Preserve—an incomparable gem of nature slated to soon become a unit of the National Park System.

When violent eruptions blew Jemez Volcano apart a million years ago, more than fifty cubic miles of rock material spewed out, covering the landscape for great distances in every direction and making the 1980 Mount Saint Helens blowout look like child's play. Valles Caldera, the almost circular grass-covered valley seen along this route, is what remains from those eruptions.

Incandescent particles that avalanched down the mountain at the end of the eruption became welded together, forming a firm but porous material called Bandelier tuff. This orange-tan light-colored rock that erodes in such strange forms will be obvious where it lines the road below Los Alamos and on the walls of Frijoles Canyon in Bandelier National Monument.

Both places—Los Alamos, on the mesa where the atomic bomb that ended World War II was developed, and Bandelier—are located on the Pajarito (little bird) Plateau, and both are well worth a short side trip to explore them.

(clockwise, top left)
The Jemez Mountain Trail
National Scenic Byway winds
through the Jemez River
valley. CCB

Cornfields on the Jemez
Pueblo Indian Reservation.
CCB

The Soda Dam on the Jemez
River. CCB

Mission ruins at Jemez State
Monument. WWD

The Pajarito Plateau has been the scene of a number of catastrophic forest fires in the past fifty years. Fifteen thousand acres burned at the upper end of Bandelier National Monument in 1977. Three times that amount of forest went up in smoke in 2000 when the Cerro Grande Fire swept through Los Alamos, and more than four hundred families lost their homes. But the worst fire

by far occurred in mid-summer of 2011. The Las Conchas Fire consumed nearly 157,000 acres, making it the largest forest fire in New Mexico's history. Evidence of all three fires is clearly visible along this route.

You can easily spend half a day or longer at Bandelier checking out the ancestral Puebloan ruins at this world-class park, which features an extensive system of self-guiding trails. Just past the town of White Rock, a short steep trail leads to the "sky city" ruin of Tsankawi, perched atop an island mesa.

By the time you descend to the Rio Grande, it's not far to Santa Fe and I-25, which will take you back to Albuquerque.

Frijoles Canyon, Bandelier National Monument. WWD

Bandelier tuff from the ancient Jemez Volcano. CCB

FINAL
THOUGHTS

Quaking Aspen. CCB

THIS BOOK HAS A BIT OF HISTORY, starting with a move in 1981 to Carlsbad, where for the next four years I would serve as Superintendent of Carlsbad Caverns National Park and Guadalupe Mountains National Park in Texas before retiring after a twenty-eight-year career with the National Park Service. During those years I was a park naturalist in many different parks and, later, a park superintendent. Throughout that time and for the seven years afterward, when I served as field biologist for The Nature Conservancy, I was regularly traveling about our state, studying and photographing its natural landscape.

Then in the late 1990s, while co-authoring two books on wild plants and their uses by New Mexico's native peoples, I was invited to join a team of scientists who were drawing up plans for a major exhibit for the New Mexico Museum of Natural History—to be located in a hall named Our Living Landscapes. Part of the thinking then called for me to write a book that would tie in with the exhibit, and so I began drafting this very book. Alas, the museum never did receive the anticipated grant that was to fund their exhibit, despite the fact that our plan had progressed to the "ready to construct" stage. And my book idea was put on hold—for the next ten years.

When writing commenced again, I realized that a great deal more photography was needed, and so I approached my botany pal and colleague of many years, Christine Bauman, who was now a professional landscape photographer in California.

So in May 2010 we made a whirlwind tour of the entire state, covering more than three thousand miles without ever leaving our borders in just ten, twelve-hour days. I was the driver, Chris, with her many cameras, lenses, and other photo gear, the photographer. That marvelous journey reinforced in me yet one more time how magical and diverse New Mexico's living landscapes truly are.

And now my wish is that you, the reader of this book, will, as you travel, also find them so.

LIST OF PLANTS

Alligator Juniper *Juniperus deppeana*

Apache Plume *Fallugia paradoxa*

Arizona Sycamore *Platanus wrightii*

Arrowleaf Balsamroot *Balsamorhiza sagittata*

Banana Yucca *Yucca baccata*

Barrel Cactus *Ferocactus wislizenii*

Big Sagebrush *Artemisia tridentata*

Bigtooth Maple *Acer grandidentatum*

Black Grama *Bouteloua eriopoda*

Blue Grama *Bouteloua gracilis*

Bluets *Hedyotis rubra*

Broom Snakeweed *Gutierrezia sarothrae*

Buffalo Grass *Buchloe dactyloides*

Button Cactus *Epithelantha micromeris*

Cane Cholla *Opuntia imbricata*

Chamisa (Rubber Rabbitbrush) *Ericameria nauseosus*

Cheatgrass *Bromus tectorum*

Chokecherry *Prunus virginiana*

Claret-cup Cactus *Echinocereus triglochidiatus*

Colorado Blue Spruce *Picea pungens*

Corkbark Fir *Abies lasiocarpa*

Creosote Bush *Larrea tridentata*

Desert Marigold *Baileya multiradiata*

Desert Willow *Chilopsis linearis*

Douglas-fir *Pseudotsuga menziesii*

Engelmann Spruce *Picea engelmannii*

Feather Indigobush *Dalea formosa*

Feltleaf Bluestar *Amsonia tharpii*

Fremont Cottonwood *Populus fremontii*

Gambel Oak *Quercus gambelii*

Honey Mesquite *Prosopis glandulosa*

Indian Paintbrush *Castilleja integra*

Indian Ricegrass *Oryzopsis hymenoides*

Limber Pine *Pinus flexilis*

Mancos Milkvetch *Astragalus humillimus*

Mexican Poppy *Eschscholzia mexicana*

Mountain Alder *Alnus tenuifolia*

Mountain Mahogany *Cercocarpus montanus*

Mulesears *Wyethia* spp.

Narrowleaf Cottonwood *Populus angustifolia*

Narrowleaf Yucca *Yucca glauca*

New Mexico Feathergrass *Stipa neomexicana*

Night-blooming Cereus *Cereus greggii*

Ocotillo *Fouquieria splendens*

One-seed Juniper *Juniperus monosperma*

Piñon Pine *Pinus edulis*

Plains Blackfoot *Melampodium leucanthum*

Ponderosa Pine *Pinus ponderosa*

Prickly Pear Cactus *Opuntia* spp.

Prince's Plume *Stanleya pinnata*

Purple Aster *Machaeranthera* spp.

Quaking Aspen *Populus tremuloides*

Rio Grande Valley Cottonwood *Populus fremontii*

Rocky Mountain Juniper *Juniperus scopulorum*

Rubber Rabbitbrush (Chamisa) *Ericameria nauseosus*

Russian Olive *Elaeagnus angustifolia*

Saguaro Cactus *Carnegiea gigantea*

Salt Cedar (Tamarisk) *Tamarix pentandra*

Sand Sagebrush *Artemisia filifolia*

Sand Verbena *Abronia angustifolia*

Scarlet Bugler *Penstemon barbatus*

Scarlet Gilia *Ipomopsis aggregata*

Scorpionweed *Phacelia corrugata*

Shinnery Oak *Quercus havardii*

Side-oats Grama *Bouteloua curtipendula*

Soaptree Yucca *Yucca elata*

Tamarisk (Salt Cedar) *Tamarix pentandra*

Three-leaf Sumac *Rhus trilobata*

Utah Juniper *Juniperus osteosperma*

White Fir *Abies concolor*

White Milkwort *Polygala alba*

Woolly Locoweed *Astragalus mollissimus*

Photograph on page 1: Bats, Carlsbad Caverns. William W. Dunmire

Project editor: Mary Wachs
Art direction: David Skolkin
Design: Jason Valdez
Maps: Deborah Reade
Manufactured in China
Library of Congress Cataloging-in-Publication Data

Dunmire, William W.
  New Mexico's living landscapes a roadside view / William W. Dunmire ; principal photography by Christine C. Bauman and William W. Dunmire.
    p. cm.
  ISBN 978-0-89013-543-3 (paperbound : alk. paper)
  1. New Mexico--Pictorial works. 2. New Mexico--Natural history--Pictorial works. 3. Landscapes--New Mexico--Pictorial works. 4. New Mexico--Description and trael. 5. Automobile travel--New Mexico. I. Bauman, Chris C. II. Title.
  F797.D86 2012
  978.9--dc23
                    2011038974

Museum of New Mexico Press
Post Office Box 2087
Santa Fe, New Mexico 87504
www.mnmpress.org